Learners' Stories: Difference and Diversity in
Language Learning

# CAMBRIDGE LANGUAGE TEACHING LIBRARY

A series covering central issues in language teaching and learning, by authors who have expert knowledge in their field.

*In this series:*

# Learners' Stories: Difference and Diversity in Language Learning

Edited by

*Phil Benson and David Nunan*

CAMBRIDGE UNIVERSITY PRESS

CAMBRIDGE UNIVERSITY PRESS
Cambridge, New York, Melbourne, Madrid, Cape Town, Singapore, São Paulo

Cambridge University Press
The Edinburgh Building, Cambridge CB2 2RU, UK

www.cambridge.org
Information on this title: www.cambridge.org/9780521614146

First published 2005

Printed in the United Kingdom at the University Press, Cambridge

*Typeface* 9/11pt Sabon    *System* QuarkXPress™

*A catalogue record for this book is available from the British Library*

ISBN–13   978-0-521-84938-8 hardback
ISBN–10   0-521-84938-1 hardback
ISBN–13   978-0-521-61414-6 paperback
ISBN–10   0-521-61414-7 paperback

# Contents

*Contents*

# Contributors

Lois Bellingham, UNITEC Institute of Technology, Auckland, NZ
Phil Benson, University of Hong Kong
Chen Jin (Brenda), Yuan Ze University, Taiwan
Chen Li-Chi (Lee), Tsing Hua National University, Taiwan
Sara Cotterall, Victoria University of Wellington, NZ
Rocío Domínguez, Ministry of Education, Peru
Zoltán Dörnyei, University of Nottingham, UK
Martin Lamb, University of Leeds, UK
Diane Malcolm, Arabian Gulf University, Bahrain
Tim Murphey, Dokkyo University, Saitama, Japan
David Nunan, University of Hong Kong
Solasa Sataporn, Sukhothai Thammathirat Open University, Thailand
Sufumi So, Carnegie Mellon University, Pittsburgh, USA
Amel Shoaib, University of Nottingham, UK
Tae Umino, Tokyo University of Foreign Studies, Japan

# Acknowledgements

We would like to thank the authors who have contributed to this volume for their trust in our ability to see their work published and for their patience in dealing with our questions and suggestions. We especially wish to thank the learners who have, both anonymously and under their own names, had the courage to share their stories with a wider audience. Lastly, thanks are due to the following individuals from Cambridge University Press: to Mickey Bonin who encouraged us to publish this volume in the first place, to Alison Sharpe and Jane Walsh, who saw the project through when Mickey left the Press, and to Jacqueline French, who copy-edited the manuscript with exceptional care and sensitivity.

Phil Benson
David Nunan

# 1  Introduction

*Phil Benson and David Nunan*

As this is a book about learners' stories, we will begin by telling the story of its origins. Several years ago, we began a research project based on interviews in which we asked university students in Hong Kong to tell us about their lifelong experiences of learning English. Many schools and universities in Hong Kong teach through the medium of English and the students that we interviewed had all begun learning English at an early age. Our aim was, therefore, simply to find out what the long-term experience of learning English 'was like' for these students. What stages did their learning pass through? What exactly did they think 'English' and 'learning English' involved at these different stages? And how did they view their experiences of second language learning within the context of their broader experiences of education and social life?

When we began the project, however, we found few points of reference for such a study in the literature on second language learning. In truth, we had only the vaguest idea of how our study connected to previous and current research. But as it progressed, we became aware that others were working along similar lines and that many were, like ourselves, working things out as they went along. For this reason, we decided to issue a call for a collection of papers that would explore the potential of research based on first-person accounts of the long-term process of learning a second language. The response took us somewhat by surprise in terms of both the number of proposals and the variety of issues and research methods involved. As we sifted through the proposals, however, we began to see the possibilities of a volume that would explore the potential of this type of research for the investigation of issues of difference and diversity in second language learning.

The significance of the '(auto)biographical' approach in the wider context of second language learning research is discussed in detail in Chapter 2. For the moment, let us note that most of the research into learner difference and diversity to date has been concerned with one overriding question. Why do individuals who presumably possess similar cognitive capacities for second language learning achieve such varied degrees of proficiency? Answers to this question have focused on the psychological and social factors involved in second language learning and, for this reason, these factors have mainly been considered from the perspective of their varied contributions to proficiency outcomes. In addition, the majority of studies have been based on experimental and survey methods aimed at isolating and scaling factors of difference and statistically correlating them with measures of proficiency.

The contributors to this volume, however, adopt a rather different perspective. In particular, they are not exclusively concerned with variable proficiency outcomes (important as this may be). Instead, they are concerned with the description of difference and diversity in a more holistic sense. In examining particular psychological and social factors, they are especially concerned with their development over time, with the relationship of these developments to the learners' broader life circumstances and goals, and with the ways in which they are influenced by the learners' active involvement in the learning process. They are, in other words, mainly interested in the question of how learners become diverse as a consequence of their long-term engagement with second languages. And it is because they wish to broaden the questions that we ask about difference and diversity that they are especially interested in learners' stories of their experiences.

The structure of this volume reflects the conventional distinction between psychological and social factors in second language learning. There is, however, a tendency to view each of these factors as being integrated with the others. Chapter 2 provides the reader with an overview of approaches to research on learner difference and diversity, with a particular emphasis on the contrast between (auto)biographical approaches and more conventional approaches in second language acquisition (SLA) research. Chapters 3 to 7 then focus on five important psychological factors – motivation, affect, age, learning strategies and identity – while Chapters 8 to 10 focus on social factors through discussion of three settings for learning – the classroom, distance learning and self-instruction.

The (auto)biographical approach to research naturally lends itself to the production of case studies of individual learning experiences. Central to these case studies are the individual learners' 'stories' of their experiences, which can be collected, analysed and represented in various ways. One important division in the (auto)biographical approach concerns the relationship between researcher(s) and the subject(s). In some studies, the researcher and subject are one person, who analyses her or his own experiences 'autobiographically'. In others, the researcher(s) analyses autobiographical data provided by others. In this case, the research is perhaps best described as 'biographical'. All of the chapters in this volume fall into the second category, although the role of the subjects varies considerably (and in one chapter the 'subject' is in fact a co-author). This volume, also, differs from another, increasingly popular form of publication in which learners' stories of their language learning are simply reproduced without analysis or comment. The different ways in which the contributors wrestle with the complex task of representing learners' stories as research is, therefore, part of the interest of this volume. Other aspects of variation include the methods of data collection (including interview, dialogue and written stories), the length of the period of learning covered, the number of subjects and the degree to which the subjects' voices are present in the final report. This variation is again part of the interest of this volume. There are, as yet, no rules for (auto)biographical research and perhaps there never will be.

The aim of this volume is not, then, to provide the reader with a comprehensive account of the role of difference and diversity in second language learning. It is, rather, to demonstrate the contribution that (auto)biography, or the analysis of learners' stories of their experiences, can make in this area. Some readers will, we feel, initially be sceptical of this contribution for reasons well rehearsed in the literature: first-person accounts of experiences tend to be 'subjective', learners lack awareness of the processes involved in their learning and their memories are apt to be unreliable. After reading this volume, however, more sceptical readers may well find that the potential drawbacks of (auto)biographical research are amply compensated by the ways in which researchers can use the stories that comprise their data to cast light on dimensions of difference and diversity that would otherwise remain concealed.

# 2 (Auto)biography and learner diversity

*Phil Benson*

The term '(auto)biography' is used in this chapter to refer to a broad approach to research that focuses on the analysis and description of social phenomena as they are experienced within the context of individual lives.[1] This approach has been widely discussed and used in the field of education, mainly as a method of exploring teachers' lives (see Casanave and Schecter 1997, and Johnson and Golombek 2002, for examples from the field of second language teacher education). The aim of this volume is to explore the potential contribution of this approach to the field of second language learning and, in particular, to the investigation of issues of learner difference and diversity. In this chapter, I will attempt to put this aim into a wider context by reviewing both the development of research on difference and diversity and the emergence of (auto)biography as an approach to second language learning research.

Before embarking on this review, however, I need to explain the sense in which I am using the terms 'difference' and 'diversity'. In a general sense, both terms can be said to refer to the same thing: the fact that people learn second languages in a variety of settings, in a variety of ways and with varied outcomes. This fact was first systematically incorporated into theories of second language learning by second language acquisition (SLA) research – a field in which 'difference' is now an established term. But 'difference' has also acquired a more specific meaning in SLA research. For SLA researchers, learners differ from each other in many ways, but most significantly in regard to the linguistic outcomes of their learning. (Auto)biographical researchers, on the other hand, tend to be concerned with both the linguistic and the non-linguistic outcomes of learning, and with the ways in which learners become different from each other in the course of the learning process. The implications of this contrast will become clearer as this chapter develops. But for the moment, I want to note that the term 'diversity' will be used here to refer to the more holistic sense in which learners differ from each other, and in preference to the term 'difference', which has become associated with a more or less exclusive focus on the variable linguistic outcomes of second language learning.

## Learner diversity in historical context

Writing of 'the tapestry of diversity in our classrooms', Murray (1996, p. 434) points to a facet of second language learning that is now at the forefront of our consciousness as teachers and researchers. The learners that we meet in our professional lives can no longer be treated as a homogeneous body. Diversity is perhaps most apparent in classrooms where the learners come from varied sociocultural and linguistic backgrounds. We have also come to recognize, however, that even learners with similar backgrounds vary in terms of the psychological predispositions and learning experiences that they bring to the classroom. We recognize, in other words, that learners are individuals and that their individuality may have significant consequences for their learning. But it is only relatively recently that the fact of learner diversity has come to our attention and, in order to understand its significance fully, we need to go back to a point where we were apparently unable to see learners at all.

### The invisible learner

An interest in learner diversity presupposes an interest in learners. The history of our field, however, shows that for much of the twentieth century researchers were far more interested in problems of teaching than they were in problems of learning. The linguists Henry Sweet and Otto Jespersen are, for example, considered to be among the 'founding fathers' of the field of second language learning research. Catford (1998, p. 467), moreover, tells us that, when he began his career in the late 1930s, their books on language teaching (Sweet 1899; Jespersen 1904) were 'among the best guides that a beginning teacher had'. Guides to good language teaching are, of course, still popular in the twenty-first century and many of them incorporate the sound advice offered by Sweet and Jespersen. Like other early authors, however, Sweet and Jespersen differ in their approach to the genre from their modern counterparts in one crucial respect. They seldom mention the learners. Indeed, it is largely the invisibility of the ubiquitous learner of present-day guides to language teaching that gives their books an 'historical' character.

One explanation for the invisibility of the learner in early research lies in its more or less exclusive concern with the application of linguistic theories that viewed language from the perspective of form and structure. These theories had considerable implications for the ways in which language learning material should be organized and presented to learners, for example, but said little about the ways in which languages were actually learned. In the late 1950s, psychology also became influential, but initially only the form of theories that viewed language learning as a behavioural response to input stimuli. Again, behaviourism offered little scope for the exploration of the learner's role in the process of second language learning. Our present-day interest in language learners is, therefore, both historically specific and relatively recent in origin. It arose, moreover, during a period in the second half of the twentieth century when diversity in the contexts and settings for second language teaching and learning was beginning to make learners far more visible than they had been in the past. We might argue, in other words, that although an interest in learner diversity presupposes an interest in learners, this interest in learners could arise only as a consequence of learner diversity itself.

## The rise of learner-focused research

By the late 1970s, 'learner-centredness' had emerged as a key concept in second language teaching based on a now largely unquestioned understanding that learners' *varied* responses to teaching are as important a factor in language learning, if not more so, than the teaching itself. In this sense, the idea of learner-centredness was a humanistic reaction to behaviourist theories that assigned little importance to the variability of learners' responses to input. The rise of learner-focused research, however, began much earlier than this, in the late 1950s, with studies on attitudes and motivation (Spolsky 2000). And in this sense, it can be viewed as an intellectual development arising from the growing influence of social psychology on second language teaching research. We might add to this that the linguistic theory on which second language teaching research could draw was also changing, in particular through the emergence of psycholinguistics and sociolinguistics, which treated language less as an abstract construct of structures and forms and more as a dynamic product of psychological and social life.

What needs to be explained, therefore, is the origin of a shift in perspective that has led to an ever more intense focus on the learner in second language research. From an intellectual perspective, we might argue that it was the consequence of a number of currents entering the field at around the same period of time. We might also consider, however, the implications of Wenden's (2002, p. 32) comment that the rise of learner-centredness 'grew out of the recognition that language learners are diverse'. Over the past 40 years or so, the expansion of institutionalized education systems, the rise in the number of individuals migrating or travelling overseas and the development of communication technologies (aspects of the phenomenon we now call 'globalization') have led to an exponential growth in the number of people studying second languages around the world. As the 'client-base' for second language education has expanded, the contexts in which individuals learn second languages have naturally become more diverse. From this perspective, it might be argued that the 'recognition of diversity' to which Wenden refers was, in fact, a recognition of an essentially new reality within second language education as a global enterprise.

It is likely, of course, that many of the aspects of learner diversity that we are now very much aware of have always existed. But it is also likely that this diversity did not simply escape the notice of researchers. The population of learners with which early-twentieth-century researchers were concerned was, in a social sense at least, far less diverse than the population that present-day researchers have to account for. We may, therefore, speculate that they failed to 'see' the learner largely because diversity was, in fact, far less visible in their classrooms than it is today. If this is the case, we have good reason to view our present-day focus on the learner as a complex and indirect intellectual response to changes in second language education that are driven primarily by a rapidly growing diversity among and within the populations of learners that second language teaching serves.

### The rise of SLA research

The emergence of SLA as a field of research that focuses on theories of second language *learning* has been one of the major outcomes of the rise of learner-focused research. This theoretical focus on learning implies a concern with learner diversity, but in order to understand the nature of this concern we must first understand the problem that the fact of learner diversity poses to second language learning theory. Rampton (1991, p. 241) argues that the major objective of SLA research has been 'to provide an account of second language learning which may then become available for fairly enduring and widespread reference by teachers and educationalists'. In order to have this widespread reference, such an account must either explicitly justify its application to all learners or explain the implications of learner diversity systematically. The SLA account of second language learning cannot, in other words, simply ignore learner diversity in the way that earlier accounts did. In response to this problem, SLA researchers largely adopted what we might call a 'two-pronged' strategy. In brief, the problem of diversity was first removed from SLA theory through the assumption of a 'universal' second language learning *process*. It then reappeared in the form of a set of *contextual* variables that might explain the different linguistic outcomes of this universal process for different groups or individuals.

## The search for SLA universals

The term 'second language learning process' is now so entrenched in the literature that it often appears to be little more than a synonym for 'second language learning' itself. It is worth recalling, however, that this term was first borrowed from the psychological literature in the early 1960s (see, for example, Rivers [1964], who was among the first to use the word 'process' in the context of second language learning). For many SLA researchers, moreover, it implies the hypothesis of a cognitive 'processing' device that transforms language input into language output. The second language learning process is, thus, often seen as an exclusively cognitive process that is both unique to language acquisition and shared by all human beings. This hypothesis has its roots in the rejection of behaviourist assumptions about second language learning and in interest in the Chomskyan conception of language as an innate property of the human mind. But it can also be seen as a theoretical response to the problems posed by the fact of learner diversity.

As Breen (2001, p. 2) argues, 'a concern for what is common among learners necessarily identifies as crucial those contributions that all learners share as human beings; contributions that exemplify their inherent biological and psychological capacities'. The need for a universal account of second language learning leads, in other words, first to an assumption that all second language learners *must* have something in common and, second, to the isolation of cognitive processing of language input as the domain within which common factors are most likely to be found. Evidence of variability in learning capacities leads the further isolation of a 'language acquisition device' within cognitive processing that is assumed to be invariable because human beings appear to share a more or less equal capacity to acquire their first languages. In a somewhat circular movement, therefore, cognitive processing comes to the forefront of accounts of the SLA account of second language learning precisely because of the need for 'enduring and widespread reference' (Rampton 1991).

The problem of learner diversity cannot simply be written off, however, because the evidence suggests that the capacity to acquire second languages is far less equally distributed than the capacity to acquire first languages. According to Long (1990, p. 661), therefore, SLA theory must answer *two* major questions:

> Which aspects of SLA are universal (presumably as a result of all learners possessing common cognitive abilities and constraints), and which aspects vary systematically as a function, for example, of age, aptitude, and attention, or of the kind of input different learners encounter?

Long's second question is, however, clearly *secondary* to the first, because, as he argues in a later paper, the focus on cognition in SLA research is not an arbitrary choice. On the contrary, it is determined by 'the very nature of the SLA beast' (Long 1997, p. 319):

> Most SLA researchers view the object of inquiry as in large part an internal, mental process: *the acquisition of new (linguistic) knowledge*. And I would say, with good reason. SLA is a process that (often) takes place in a social setting, of course, but then so do most internal processes . . . and that neither obviates the need for theories of those processes, nor shifts the goal of inquiry to a theory of the settings. (ibid., italics in original)

This reduction of the SLA 'object of inquiry' to its cognitive essences is significant because it legitimizes the attempt to produce a universally applicable account of second language learning in the face of evidence of diversity. In particular, it reduces the theoretical problems posed by learner diversity to manageable proportions. Since the second language learning *process* is invariable almost by definition, learner diversity can have few implications for it. It may, however, have implications for the *linguistic outcomes* of this process, which clearly vary from individual to individual. Moreover, if diversity is not a property of the internal mental processes involved in second language learning, it can only be a property of something external to them. For SLA researchers, therefore, diversity becomes a property of the *contexts* in which the learning process occurs.

### The SLA perspective on learner diversity

Several recent critiques of SLA research have referred to a tendency to treat variability in second language learning as secondary to its universal characteristics. Larsen-Freeman (2001, p. 12), for example, points out that, 'while the learner has not been ignored in second language acquisition (SLA) research, more attention has been paid to characterizing an acquisition process that is common to all learners'. Although SLA researchers recognize that success in second language learning is variable, she argues, it has been 'left to the research on individual learner factors to explain this differential success' (ibid.). As Larsen-Freeman's review of research shows, however, these factors have nevertheless been the subject of a considerable body of work. An emphasis on the secondary status of this work may therefore lead us to overlook the particular ways in which the concept of difference (the established term in SLA research) has been constructed.

The SLA approach to the question of difference dates back to Schumann (1978a, 1978b), who aimed to make sense of the various factors involved in second language learning through his 'pidginization hypothesis' (later known as the 'acculturation model'). Schumann (1978b) began with a taxonomy of factors of variability identified in the research to date but immediately noted that, although such taxonomies were valuable, 'it is necessary to determine which factor or set of factors are more important in that they *cause* second-language acquisition to occur' (ibid., p. 27, italics in original). He then hypothesized that factors of social and psychological distance from speakers of the target language were likely to be among the most important causal factors and, indeed, that 'the learner will acquire the second language only to the degree that he acculturates' in a social and psychological sense (ibid., p. 28).

The relationship of Schumann's acculturation model to the hypothesis of a universal language acquisition device was not explicitly stated and remains problematic. In describing acquisition as 'a by-product of acculturation', Schumann (1978b, p. 46) seems to imply that second language learning is a social and psychological (and thus inherently variable) process. But as Larsen-Freeman (1983, p. 7) described Schumann's model, it had 'no cognitive element in it' because Schumann believed that 'given social and psychological integration, an individual endowed with normal brain faculty will acquire a second language'. Whether Schumann, in fact, believed this or not is a moot point. With hindsight, however, we can see how his attempt to model causality in SLA set an agenda for research in the field of 'individual differences' that has largely been concerned with the influence of contextual factors on 'differential success' (Larsen-Freeman 2001).

This emphasis on the articulation of relationships between contextual factors and the linguistic outcomes of second language learning is illustrated by Ellis's (1994, p. 197) formulation of the problem of learner difference:

> Learners differ enormously in how quickly they learn an L2, in the type of proficiency they acquire (for example, conversational ability as opposed to literacy in the L2) and the ultimate level of proficiency they reach. In part these differences can be explained by reference to psychological factors such as language aptitude, learning style and personality . . . but in part they are socially determined.

As Ellis's review of research shows, psychological factors such as language aptitude, learning style, age, motivation, strategy use and learner beliefs, and social factors such as gender, class, ethnicity, cultural background and settings for learning have all been extensively investigated (see also Skehan 1989, 1991; Gardner 1997; Larsen-Freeman 2001; Dörnyei and Skehan 2003; Siegel 2003; Barkhuizen 2004; Ellis 2004).

The notion of 'context' tends to be ill-defined in the literature. The psychological research, for example, tends to identify context with social and situational setting alone. But non-linguistic psychological processes also tend to be treated as contextual to processes specifically directed at linguistic input. The emphasis on the correlation of both social and non-linguistic psychological factors with linguistic outcomes is also clear.

Within both branches of the research there has also been a strong emphasis on the use of quantitative experimental and survey methods to isolate and scale psychological and sociological 'variables' and correlate them with linguistic outcomes (most often measured in terms of proficiency level or gain). The use of the quantitative methods, it could be argued, offers the possibility of an account of the role of learner diversity in terms of the systematic and regular influence of contextual variables on the outcomes of an essentially invariable cognitive process. The fragmentation of the research, however, means that in practice this remains a distant goal. Ellis (1994, p. 524), for example, concluded his review of the research on factors of difference with the comment that it 'has told us little about the relative strength of different learner factors or how they interrelate'. He also reiterated Skehan's (1991, p. 524) call for 'naturalistic' studies that 'can shed light on the individuality of single learners and can also show the dynamic nature of the interaction between the malleable aspects of individual difference (for example, anxiety and motivation) and learners' learning experiences'. More recently, Larsen-Freeman (2001, p. 24) concluded her review of research in a similar fashion with a call for 'more holistic research that links integrated individual difference research from emic and etic perspectives to the processes, mechanisms and conditions of learning within different contexts over time'.

In the light of these calls for a more 'naturalistic' or 'holistic' approach to research, it is worth noting that Schumann's acculturation model was largely based on empirical evidence derived from case studies based on first-person accounts of second language learning. The comments in this section, however, raise the question of what the objectives of such case studies should be. Although SLA research tells us a good deal about the factors that 'make up' learner diversity, its treatment of these factors as 'contextual' has generated certain blind spots in the research. As Norton and Toohey (2001, p. 308) point out, SLA research tends to view context only as a 'modifier' of the internal activity involved in language learning. And because the factors involved in learner diversity are removed to the domain of context in SLA research, they too are viewed primarily as modifiers of cognitive processing that are ultimately channelled through the linguistic input that learners receive. As a result, little attention is paid to the ways in which these factors *develop* over time or as a consequence of individual experiences of language learning, and even less attention has been paid to the sense in which they might be considered as outcomes of the second language learning process in their own right.

## (Auto)biographical research

The emphasis on the search for cognitive universals in SLA research has been at the centre of a number of recent critiques (Pennycook 1990; Rampton 1991, 1997; Block 1996b, 2003; Lantolf 1996; Firth and Wagner 1997; Tarone 1997; Ellis 1999; Pavlenko and Lantolf 2000; Breen 2001; Lantolf and Pavlenko 2001; Norton and Toohey 2001). These critiques have also argued, from a variety of theoretical perspectives, for a greater emphasis on qualitative research directed at the holistic description of second language learning experiences and for a greater emphasis on the social, affective and conceptual dimensions of the learning process. In the context of these critiques, Norton and Toohey (2001, p. 310) refer to a relatively recent literature concerned 'not only with studying individuals acting on L2 input and producing L2 output, but also with studying how L2 learners are situated in specific social, historical, and cultural contexts and how learners resist or accept the positions those contexts offer them'.

In the following sections I will review two major strands within this literature. The first strand can be described as 'autobiographical' in the sense that it involves first-person analysis of experiences of second language learning by those who directly experience them. The second can be described as 'biographical' in the sense that it involves third-person analysis of the experiences of others.

### Autobiographical research

Autobiographical research first appeared in the second language learning literature in the form of 'introspective diary studies' – a mode of research in which diaries or journals recorded over relatively long periods of time are analysed from a variety of perspectives (e.g., Schumann and Schumann 1977; Rivers 1979; Bailey 1980, 1983; Schumann 1980; Schmidt and Frota 1986; Jones 1994; Campbell 1996; Leung 2002). As Nunan (1992, p. 115) points out, this mode of research was initially seen as a means of gaining 'insights into the mental processes underlying observable behaviour'. It is now recognized, however, that the strength of diary studies lies more in the fact that researchers are able 'to tap into affective factors, language learning strategies, and the learners' own perception' (Bailey and Nunan 1996, p. 197). Similarly, an emphasis on the close analysis of linguistic data in earlier studies (e.g., Schmidt and Frota 1986) has given way to a much greater emphasis on the social and psychological dimensions of language learning (e.g., Campbell 1996).

Although the number of published studies remains relatively small, introspective diary study has become an established research method informed by principles designed to increase reliability and validity (Bailey 1983, 1991; Bailey and Ochsner 1983). Paramount among these principles is an insistence that the data should be recorded concurrently with the learning. Adherence to this principle, however, usually means that researchers must decide to collect the data in advance and complete the data collection within a relatively short period of time. For this reason, published studies tend to cover periods of a year or less in which the researchers study a second language for the purposes of the research, or at least in the knowledge that research will be one of the outcomes.

In the light of this limitation, attention has shifted in recent years to recollection as a means of exploring longer-term experiences of language learning in more 'authentic' settings. Particular interest has been shown in language learning 'memoirs' from beyond the SLA literature, written both by second language researchers and others (e.g., Wierzbicka 1985; Hoffman 1989; Kaplan 1993; Lvovich 1997; Ogulnick 1998). From a conventional point of view, memoirs are something less than 'research'. Kaplan (1994), however, comments that she viewed writing her own memoir as an alternative to the research methods she had encountered in her reading of the SLA literature. Cameron (2000, p. 91) also argues that memoirs are worth studying because they particularly demonstrate 'the strength of feelings stirred up by language learning':

> They make clear, for instance, that the acquisition of a new language raises questions of subjectivity and desire: the problems confronted by the learner are not just technical or mechanical ('how do I say X in this language?'), but involve complex issues of identity ('who am I when I speak this language?', or alternatively 'can I be "me" when I speak this language?')

Nevertheless memoirs retain a somewhat equivocal status as research and they have entered the SLA literature mainly as a source of data for third-person analysis in work on questions of identity in the memoirs of immigrants to North America (Morrow 1997; Pavlenko 1998, 2001a, 2001b, 2001c; Pavlenko and Lantolf 2000; and Lantolf and Pavlenko 2001).

The most significant consequence of this interest in language learning memoirs, however, has been the emergence of autobiographical recollection within the second language teaching and learning literature itself.

Oxford and Green (1996), for example, have argued for the value of 'learning histories' as a source of data for discussion and reflection in the classroom (see also Aoki 2002; Horwitz *et al.* 1997, 2004), while others have viewed them as examples from which teachers and learners can acquire knowledge of the processes involved in successful learning. The aim of Belcher and Connor's (2001, p. 2) collection of individually and collaboratively produced language-learning autobiographies, for example, was mainly to help 'others to understand better how advanced second-language literacy can be achieved' (see also Stevick 1989; Murphey 1997, 1998a, 1998b; Ogulnick 2000). Recollection was also proposed as a research technique by Cohen and Scott (1996) and Oxford *et al.* (1996). At that time, however, they were unable to cite any published examples of its use. Autobiographical recollection has, however, recently been used by He (2002) to investigate learning strategies. It has also been used in research on second language literacy (Shen 1989; Bell 1995, 1997; Connor 1999), motivation (Lim 2002), autonomy and self-directed learning (Brown 2002; Benson, Chik and Lim 2003; Walker 2004), bilingual parenting (Fries 1998; Kouritzin 2000a), and the experiences of non-native speakers as learners and teachers (Lin *et al.* 2002; Sakui 2002). In these studies, the drawback of 'inevitable memory deterioration between the language learning experience and the research study' (Cohen and Scott 1996, p. 102) tends to be counterbalanced by the researchers' intimate knowledge of the contexts of their own learning and by the insights that are gained from a longer-term view of the learning process.

### Biographical research

One of the chief limitations of autobiographical research lies in the fact that the researcher-subject must be able to write a publishable account of her or his own learning experiences. Biographical research thus opens up the possibility of exploring, albeit indirectly, the experiences of a much wider range of learners. As in the case of autobiographical research, in the following review I will make a broad distinction between studies based on concurrent data and studies based on recollection.

Biographical research in the field of second language learning can be traced back to a series of longitudinal case studies related to Schumann's (1978a, 1978b) pidginization hypothesis, or acculturation model (e.g., Cazden *et al.* 1975; Shapira 1978; Kessler and Idar 1979; Schmidt 1983). Although these studies were largely structured around the analysis of linguistic performance data, they differed from other case studies published at around the same time in the significant use they made of information about the subjects' life experiences. For example, in Schmidt's (1983) three-year study of Wes – a Japanese artist who had acquired English with little formal instruction – the main source of data consisted of 21 hours of audio-taped speech. The analysis of this audio data is organized in terms of categories of grammatical, discourse and sociolinguistic competence, but Schmidt's (1983, p. 145) 'extensive but irregular field notes' also play a significant explanatory role throughout.

In more recent case studies – often described by their authors as 'ethnographic' – biographical data play a more prominent role, influencing both the degree of emphasis on linguistic developments and the structure of the published work (e.g., Gillette 1994; Polanyi 1995; McKay and Wong 1996; Lam 2000; Norton 2000, 2001; Toohey 2000; Teutsch-Dwyer 2001; Chen 2002; Newcombe 2002). Among these, Teutsch-Dwyer's (2001) study of the morphosyntactic development in the English of Karol – a Polish immigrant to the USA who had also acquired English with little formal instruction – is closest in conception to Schmidt's (1983) study of Wes. But the fact that Teutsch-Dwyer explains linguistic developments in Karol's English through the story of his immigration to the USA and his relationship with a female partner marks a significant difference between the two papers.

In other studies, linguistic developments are more broadly sketched out and sometimes constitute little more than a statement of the problem to be explored. Gillette (1994), for example, used proficiency assessments to identify three 'effective' and three 'ineffective' learners, but the bulk of her study is concerned with the exploration of relationships between life goals and strategy use based on ethnographic and biographical data. Similarly, Polanyi's (1995) study, based on narratives written by American study-abroad students in Russia, seeks to explain differences between male and female assessed proficiency gains, but the main focus of the paper falls upon an analysis of the gendered nature of the study-abroad experience for many female students.

In some recent studies, non-linguistic outcomes are the major focus of attention. Swain and Miccoli's (1994) study of an adult Japanese learner's participation in a course on collaborative learning, for example, is mainly concerned with the learner's affective development during the course, while Allen's (1996) study of an adult Libyan learner is concerned with the evolution of his beliefs about language learning during an English for Academic Purposes (EAP) course. Block's (1996a; 1998) case studies of language learning classrooms focus upon the learners' interpretations and evaluations of classroom events and processes rather than developments in their language proficiency. The language-based longitudinal case study of the late 1970s has thus evolved gradually into a more 'ethnographic' form, in which the description of language learning experiences and their non-linguistic outcomes plays an increasingly important role.

Biography properly speaking, however, has been the province of 'life history' research, which is usually based, in the context of second language learning, on recollective data collected either through interviews or in the form of written essays. Evans' (1988) book-length study of the experiences of university-level foreign language students and teachers in the UK appears to be the earliest example of life history interviewing in the field of second language learning. The aims of Evans' study – to 'understand the experience of a group and articulate it' (ibid., p. 1) – were relatively open-ended and the editors of this book adopted a similarly open-ended approach in research into the lifelong language learning experiences of university-level learners of English in Hong Kong (Benson and Nunan 2004). The objective in each case was to paint a contextually rich picture of the experience of learning, which took account of both the commonalities of the setting and the specificities of individual experiences of it.

Other life history studies have focused on specific questions concerned with affect and cognition (Oxford 1996), motivational development (Spolsky 2000), language loss among Asian-American immigrants (Hinton 2001), access to ESL classes for immigrant women in Canada (Kouritzin 2000c), language policy in China (Lam 2002) and multilingual identities of Asian learners of English (Kanno 2000, 2003; Benson, Chik and Lim 2003; Block 2002). Life histories, typically collected in the form of short essays, have also been used as a source of data for more abstract theoretical work (Schumann 1997; Tse 2000; Carter 2002). In Schumann's recent work, for example, 'linguistic autobiographies' written by his students form part of a data set (which also includes published introspective diary studies and language memoirs) supporting an explanation of variable success in second language learning in terms of 'preferences and aversions acquired in the lifetime of the individual' (1997, p. 36).

## The rise of (auto)biographical research?

In this brief literature review I have extracted a relatively small number of studies from the many thousands that have been published in the field of second language learning over the past 25 years or so and brought them together under the heading of '(auto)biographical research'. In doing so, I am attempting to establish what Golden-Biddle and Locke (1997, p. 29) call a 'synthesized coherence' by claiming that these studies constitute a coherent body of work in spite of the fact that they are in many ways unrelated to each other. What is it, then, that ties these studies together and differentiates them from others, and what is it about them that justifies the use of the term '(auto)biographical'?

Reviews of the contents of the major journals in our field suggest that, although qualitative research remains a minority interest, it is nevertheless gaining ground (Lazaraton 2000; Gao, Li and Lu 2001). To describe the studies reviewed here as 'qualitative' would therefore be one way of separating them from the majority and, especially, from the bulk of studies in the SLA research tradition discussed earlier. Qualitative inquiry, however, covers a variety of approaches and the scope of the studies reviewed here can be further narrowed down by contrasting them with (a) qualitative studies of learning activities (such as think aloud studies of learners working on tasks of various kinds) and (b) qualitative studies of learning situations (such as observational studies or classroom ethnographies). In contrast to these types, the studies I am concerned with here are (a) based upon first-person accounts of relatively long-term processes of learning and (b) focused on learners and their experiences rather than the learning activities or situations in which they participate. Many of these studies are case studies of individual learners or, more narrowly, studies of the sense that is made of learning experiences as learners participate in a variety of activities and situations over relatively long periods of time.

A second way of identifying this body of work, however, would be to point to its connections to parallel work concerned with narratives of experience in other fields. As Lieblich, Tuval-Mashiach and Zilber (1998, p. 3) show, narrative-based studies have flourished since the mid-1980s in a variety of fields, including psychology, gender studies, education, anthropology, sociology, linguistics, law and history. The influence of this work has, moreover, been such that some researchers have written of a 'biographical turn' in the social sciences (Chamberlayne, Bornat and Wengraf 2000; Roberts 2002), while the title of one book goes so far as to suggest that we are now living in a 'biographical age' (Goodley *et al.* 2004). According to Roberts (2002, p. 1), biographical research 'seeks to understand the changing experiences and outlooks of individuals in their daily lives, what they see as important, and how to provide interpretations of the accounts they give of their past, present and future'. This would also be an apt description of the research I have reviewed and, although it would probably be overstating the case to claim that second language learning research is also on the verge of an (auto)biographical 'turn', it is worth noting that several of the more recent studies make explicit reference to biographical research in the social sciences and that discussions of narrative and life history methods have begun to appear in the literature (Kouritzin 2000b; Bell 2002; Pavlenko 2002).

The term '(auto)biographical research' would seem to apply most appropriately, then, to recent studies in which there is an explicit attempt to collect and analyse learners' stories of learning experiences using methods and frameworks developed in the social sciences. When we look at earlier work such as the introspective diary studies and case studies of the late 1970s, however, we see very similar goals and methods at work. This suggests that the roots of current interest in (auto)biography as a research tool are partly indigenous and certainly deeper than they appear at first sight. It also points to a possible underlying shift in focus within the field from 'the learner' as an abstract, or universalized, construct to actual learners and their historically and contextually situated experiences of learning.

## (Auto)biography and learner diversity

Earlier in this chapter, I suggested that the shift from language-focused to learner-focused research could perhaps be explained by the growing visibility of learner diversity as a factor in late-twentieth-century language education. For what reason, then, could we now be on the verge of a further shift in focus to the learner as an individual? One possible reason could be that SLA research has so far significantly failed to explain the consequences of learner diversity for the learning process. In the remainder of this chapter, however, I want to look more closely at the origins of the 'biographical turn' in the social sciences and, in particular, at the possibility that diversity in second language learning has taken on an essentially new character that cannot readily be explained in terms of the influence of contextual variables on the linguistic outcomes of the learning process.

Some evidence for this 'new' character of learner diversity can be found in Rustin's (2000) discussion of the relationship between the biographical turn and the changing nature of the social processes that social scientists investigate. Drawing on the work of Giddens (1991) and other contemporary social theorists on 'individualization' as a characteristic process of late modern society, Rustin (2000, p. 33) contrasts the situation of modernity, in which individual identities were largely determined by 'social scripts', and the situation of late modernity, in which 'contemporary societies throw more and more responsibility on to individuals to choose their own identities'. In contemporary society, he argues:

> Social structures – classes, extended families, occupational communities, long-term employment within a firm – which formerly provided strong frames of identity, grow weaker. Simultaneously, society exposes individuals to bombardments of information, alternative versions of how life might be lived, and requires of individuals that they construct an 'authentic' version of themselves, making use of the numerous identity-props which consumer-society makes available.

18

In the context of these changes, he suggests, 'the time seems right for a fresh methodological turn towards the study of individuals, a turn to biography' (ibid., p. 34).

Extending this argument to the field of second language learning research, we might argue that 'individualization' is the reverse side of the coin of 'globalization' and the breakdown of language-based cultural frames of reference for identity that accompanies greater global mobility for individuals. There are clear parallels between the assumption that diversity in second language learning is contextually determined and the assumption that individual identities are determined by relatively fixed sociocultural locations. More importantly, we can perhaps see how second language learning is implicated in processes of 'individualization' on a global scale. Second language learning can be seen both as a contributory factor to global mobility and the breakdown of 'first language' identities and as part of the process by which individuals construct new linguistic identities for themselves – see, for example, Benson, Chik and Lim (2003) and Block (2002) on the multilingual identities of Asian learners of English. In a world in which the boundaries between sociocultural contexts are increasingly blurred, learner diversity indeed appears to take on a new character, in which the construction of new, and often highly individualized, multilingual identities *through* second language learning plays a crucial role.

In the context of these changes, the reduction of the object of inquiry of SLA research to the mental processes that produce linguistic knowledge (Long 1997, p. 319) appears to be especially problematic. Kasper (1997, p. 309), for example, defends this reduction as a *necessary* abstraction from 'the complex multiple identities of real people' and states that she is comfortable with an essentially cognitivist definition of the language learning process, 'because in the final analysis, learning or acquiring anything is about establishing new knowledge structures and making that knowledge available for effective and efficient use' (ibid., p. 310). This statement, however, conceals the extent to which 'the complex multiple identities of real people' may be a significant non-linguistic outcome of language learning. SLA research does, of course, take account of factors of identity in the explanation of the variable outcomes of learning, but by treating them as contextual factors it misses important opportunities to investigate the interaction of the linguistic and non-linguistic dimension of the second language learning process. As Lantolf and Pavlenko (2001, p. 145) suggest, 'learners actively engage in constructing the terms and conditions of their own learning'. This implies a view of the learning process in which the contextual variables of SLA research are seen as both determinants and outcomes of the learning process. It is perhaps, however, only in the light of recent discussions of individualization as a characteristic social process of late modernity that it has become possible to view contexts of learning in this way.

(Auto)biographical research has certain clear advantages in investigations of learner diversity in its new guises, because it allows us to see how psychological and social contexts of learning can develop over time. Indeed, it is only through access to learners' stories of their experiences that we are able to see how they become different from each other as their learning progresses. Learner diversity, in its late-modern guise, appears to be largely a matter of the construction of diverse identities through second language learning and, as Lieblich, Tuval-Mashiach and Zilber (1998, p. 7) argue, from the perspective of one strand of (auto)biographical research 'personal narratives, in both facets of content and form, *are* people's identities' (italics in original).

As Pavlenko and Lantolf (2000, p. 13) point out, however, earlier work (introspective diary studies especially) tended to focus on 'people whose goal seems to be restricted to developing some degree of proficiency in language as a code, but not to cross the border into the domain where selves and worlds are reconstructed'. Their own work, on the other hand, focuses on this second type of learner, or 'the atypical experience of adults who attempt to become native speakers of their second language' (ibid., p. 162). (Auto)biography, then, appears to be particularly suited to the investigation of learners whose experiences of language learning involve 'border crossings' – both geographical and psychological – and the construction of new second language identities. We may well ask, however, whether the growing visibility of such 'atypical' learners in research could lead to a new view of the more 'typical' learner. It may well be the case that all second language learners tackle issues of identity in the sense that any effort to learn a second language involves decisions about the ways in which it will be learned and the consequences that it will have for the learner.

## Conclusion

The aim of this chapter has been to set the scene for this volume by establishing the relationship between (auto)biographical research and the issue of learner diversity. I have also suggested, however, that learner diversity is rather more than an 'issue' in second language learning research. The nature of learner diversity is changing and the ways in which it is changing are likely to have a fundamental influence on the ways in which we conceptualize second language learning research. Research to date has established a number of important dimensions of diversity – motivation, affect, age, strategy use, setting and so on. These have, however, largely been viewed as static contextual factors that influence, but are not influenced by, the learning process. (Auto)biographical research is beginning to show, however, the sense in which these factors are integral and dynamic dimensions of second language learning that are intimately tied up with the construction of identity. The chapters that follow approach these factors from this point of view and, in doing so, they offer a perspective on learner diversity, I would argue, that is particularly fitting to the realities of second language education that are now before us.

## Note

1. The term '(auto)biography' here refers to both biography and autobiography. Other terms used in the literature include 'narrative research' (Polkinghorne 1988; Bruner 1990, 1991; Riessman 1993; Lieblich, Tuval-Mashiach and Zilber 1998), 'narrative study of lives' (Josselson and Lieblich 1993), 'life history' (Bertaux 1981; Goodson and Sikes 2002), 'biography' (Chamberlayne, Bornat and Wengraf 2000; Roberts 2002; Goodley *et al.* 2004), 'autoethnography' (Ellis and Bochner 2000) and 'personal experience' (Clandinin and Connelly 1994). Roberts (2002) includes autobiography under the heading of biography. He also uses the term 'auto/biography' on occasion. I use the term '(auto)biography' to indicate that, in the context of second language learning research, the data are as a rule first-person (autobiographical) accounts of experience that are analysed either by the subject of the research (autobiographically) or by another researcher (biographically).

# 3 Affect in lifelong learning: Exploring L2 motivation as a dynamic process

*Amel Shoaib and Zoltán Dörnyei*

The study reported in this paper addresses a largely uncharted area within motivation research, the temporal progression of student motivation over a longer period within the lifespan. A qualitative research approach involving 25 interviews was used to identify and document different motivational influences and various temporal patterns in language learners over a period of about two decades. The method of data analysis employed in our study followed a qualitative 'template approach' (Miles and Huberman 1984, 1994; Crabtree and Miller 1992). According to this approach, large volumes of text are coded, using an 'analysis guide' or 'template', so that segments about an identified topic (the codes) can be assembled into larger themes as part of the interpretive analytical process. The use of this approach resulted in several insights into the temporal progression of motivation, some of which have not been afforded much attention in the literature before. The paper concludes by discussing implications for future work in this novel area of research.

## Motivation to learn a foreign language

Research on language learning motivation was first initiated and then consistently pursued by Robert Gardner and his associates in Canada (e.g., Gardner and Lambert 1959, 1972; Gardner and MacIntyre 1991, 1993; Tremblay and Gardner 1995; Gardner, Tremblay and Masgoret 1997; Clément and Gardner 2001; Gardner 2001). These researchers have adopted a social-psychological perspective and developed a motivational theory centred around language attitudinal variables and firmly grounded in empirical data obtained through scientific research procedures using standardized assessment instruments.

In the 1990s, drawing on the Canadian initiative, there was a broadening of perspectives in second language (L2) motivational research, exploring a number of different motivational dimensions that were largely 'imported' from both educational research and the psychology of learning (for reviews, see Dörnyei 1998, 2001a). This 'cross-fertilization' led to an unprecedented boom in L2 motivation studies; a variety of new models and approaches were put forward in the literature, resulting in what Gardner and Tremblay (1994) have called a 'motivational renaissance'. A common feature of these new research attempts was the move towards a more *situated approach* to the study of motivation, examining how the immediate learning context influences the learners' overall disposition and how motivation, in turn, affects concrete learning processes within a classroom context. It was argued by several researchers (e.g., Julkunen 1989; Brown 1990; Crookes and Schmidt 1991; Dörnyei 1994; Oxford and Shearin 1994) that the classroom environment had a much stronger motivational impact than had been proposed before, highlighting the significance of motives associated with the L2 course, teacher and learner group. It is interesting to note that this change in thinking in the L2 field was parallel to a similar shift in educational psychology towards a more grounded and contextualized approach to motivation research (e.g., Stipek 1996; Hickey 1997; Wentzel 1999).

The situated approach soon drew attention to another, rather neglected, aspect of motivation: its *dynamic character* and *temporal variation*. As Dörnyei (2000, 2001a) has argued, when motivation is examined in its relationship to specific learner behaviours and classroom processes, there is a need to adopt a *process-oriented approach* that can account for the daily 'ups and downs' of motivation to learn, that is, the ongoing changes of motivation over time. Looking at it from this perspective, motivation is not seen as a static attribute but rather as a dynamic factor that displays continuous fluctuation, going through certain ebbs and flows. Indeed, even during a single L2 course one can notice that language learning motivation shows a certain amount of changeability, and in the context of learning a language for several years, or over a lifetime, motivation is expected to go through very diverse phases.

## Motivational change over time

The study of the temporal aspects of student motivation is not without antecedents in the psychological literature; we can find examples of work that has incorporated certain elements of time into the research paradigms (cf. Karniol and Ross 1996; Covington 1998; Husman and Lens 1999), but the focus of the research along these lines has typically been on general issues such as past attributions or future goals. The most important impact in this area has come from the work of the German psychologists Heinz Heckhausen and Julius Kuhl (e.g., Heckhausen 1991; Heckhausen and Kuhl 1985), who constructed a process theory of motivation, which is often referred to as the *Action Control Theory*. This theory is based on the assumption that there are distinct temporally ordered phases within the motivational process, most importantly:

1. the *'predecisional phase'*, which can be seen as the decision-making stage of motivation, involving complex planning and goal-setting processes during which initial wishes and desires are articulated and evaluated in terms of their desirability and chance of fulfilment, and subsequently goals and intentions are formed;
2. the *'postdecisional phase'*, which is the implementational stage of motivation, involving motivational maintenance and control mechanisms during the enactment of the intention that determine action initiation and perseverance, and which help to overcome various internal obstacles to action.

Heckhausen and Kuhl believed that these two phases were energized and directed by largely different motives. As Heckhausen (1991, p. 163) concluded, 'Why one wants to do something and that one wants to do it is one thing, but its actual implementation and successful completion is another.'

The importance of a temporal perspective and the notion of various motivational phases has also been recognized in the field of second language acquisition. Williams and Burden (1997, p. 121), for example, separated three stages of the motivation process along a continuum: 'Reasons for doing something' → 'Deciding to do something' → 'Sustaining the effort, or persisting'. As they argued, the first two stages involved *initiating* motivation whereas the third stage involved *sustaining* motivation, and this distinction bears a close resemblance to Heckhausen and Kuhl's theory. Similarly, Ushioda (1996, 2001) has also emphasized that when it comes to institutionalized learning, the common experience appears to be motivational flux rather than stability, which warrants the 'notion of a temporal frame of reference shaping motivational thinking' (Ushioda 1998, p. 82). She argued that, in order to uncover the intricacies of the temporal dimension, a more qualitative research approach should be adopted instead of the traditional, questionnaire-based quantitative approach.

How can we operationalize the notion of motivational development? In response to this challenge, Dörnyei and Ottó (1998) have put forward an elaborate conceptualization of the temporal aspect of motivation (see also Dörnyei 2000, 2001a). Their model synthesizes a number of different lines of research in a unified framework, detailing how initial wishes and desires are first transformed into goals and then into operationalized intentions, and how these intentions are enacted, leading (hopefully) to the accomplishment of the goal and concluded by the final evaluation of the process. Following Heckhausen and Kuhl, they suggested that from a temporal perspective at least three distinct phases of the motivational process should be separated:

1. *Preactional stage:* First, motivation needs to be *generated* – the motivational dimension related to this initial phase can be referred to as *choice motivation*, because the generated motivation leads to the selection of the goal or task that the individual will pursue.

2. *Actional stage:* Second, the generated motivation needs to be actively *maintained* and *protected* while the particular action lasts. This motivational dimension has been referred to as *executive motivation*, and it is particularly relevant to sustained activities such as studying an L2 and to learning in classroom settings, where students are exposed to a great number of distracting influences, such as off-task thoughts, irrelevant distractions from others, anxiety about the tasks, or physical conditions that make it difficult to complete the task.

3. *Postactional stage:* Finally, there is a third phase following the completion of the action – termed *motivational retrospection* – which concerns the learners' *retrospective evaluation* of how things went. The way students process their past experiences in this retrospective phase will determine the kind of activities they will be motivated to pursue in the future.

Figure 3.1 summarizes the main motives that influence the learner's behaviour/thinking during the three motivational phases. These motives include many of the well-known concepts described both in the psychological and L2 literature (for a detailed discussion, see Dörnyei 2001a). What is important to note about the lists of relevant motives is that – in accordance with Heckhausen and Kuhl's claim – the different motivational phases appear to be fuelled by largely different motives.

The research reported in this paper was inspired by the process-oriented approach outlined above, but the direction of this research was different from earlier studies. Rather than looking at how motivation is generated, sustained and after the completion of the action analysed, we took a broader perspective and examined how motivation evolved over a longer period of time. Thus, our study concerns the macro-processes that are involved in motivational dynamics. This approach ventures into uncharted territories (for a recent exception, see Lim 2002) but is not without parallel in contemporary motivational psychology; during the past few years a number of researchers have started to frame motivational development within a broad, lifespan perspective, for example J. Heckhausen's (2000) work on 'developmental regulation across the life span' and Smith and Spurling's (2001) research on 'motivation for lifelong learning'.

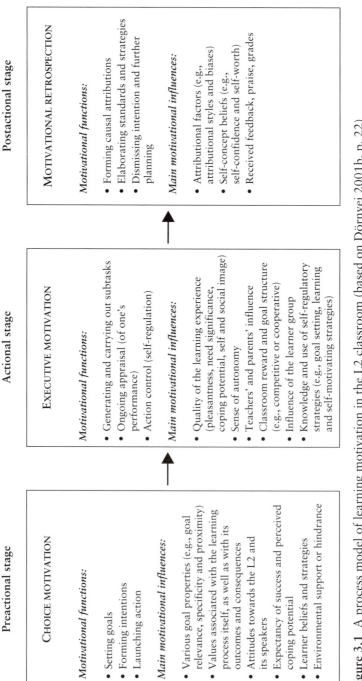

**Preactional stage**

**CHOICE MOTIVATION**

*Motivational functions:*

- Setting goals
- Forming intentions
- Launching action

*Main motivational influences:*

- Various goal properties (e.g., goal relevance, specificity and proximity)
- Values associated with the learning process itself, as well as with its outcomes and consequences
- Attitudes towards the L2 and its speakers
- Expectancy of success and perceived coping potential
- Learner beliefs and strategies
- Environmental support or hindrance

**Actional stage**

**EXECUTIVE MOTIVATION**

*Motivational functions:*

- Generating and carrying out subtasks
- Ongoing appraisal (of one's performance)
- Action control (self-regulation)

*Main motivational influences:*

- Quality of the learning experience (pleasantness, need significance, coping potential, self and social image)
- Sense of autonomy
- Teachers' and parents' influence
- Classroom reward and goal structure (e.g., competitive or cooperative)
- Influence of the learner group
- Knowledge and use of self-regulatory strategies (e.g., goal setting, learning and self-motivating strategies)

**Postactional stage**

**MOTIVATIONAL RETROSPECTION**

*Motivational functions:*

- Forming causal attributions
- Elaborating standards and strategies
- Dismissing intention and further planning

*Main motivational influences:*

- Attributional factors (e.g., attributional styles and biases)
- Self-concept beliefs (e.g., self-confidence and self-worth)
- Received feedback, praise, grades

**Figure 3.1** A process model of learning motivation in the L2 classroom (based on Dörnyei 2001b, p. 22)

## The study

*Participants*

The participants of our in-depth interview study included 15 female and 10 male participants, all between the ages of 18 and 34. These interviewees were of mixed nationalities (European, Asian and Middle Eastern) and were selected on the basis that they were young non-native learners of English known by the interviewers who were actively engaged in developing their English proficiency either by themselves or through institutionalized learning. They all had a working knowledge of English but showed some variance in terms of how advanced their competence was.

*Interviewers*

The interviews were conducted by a group of research assistants who were recruited from two specialization courses at the School of English Studies, University of Nottingham. In the end, 25 of a total of 47 interviews were used for the purpose of the study. We selected only those interviews in which the interviewers were skilled in the way they conducted their interviews and knowledgeable in the topic being investigated; they had good conversational skills; and they had generated sufficiently long interviews that contained rich data about the interviewees and the cause of their motivational change. We discarded interviews if it was felt that they were rushed; the interviewers did not encourage their interviewees to talk about their motivational change but concentrated instead on general motivational issues; the interviewers asked leading or loaded questions; and lastly the interviewee was over the age limit set for this study (over 34 years of age).

*Interview procedures*

A semi-structured interview type was adopted for the study, involving a relatively fixed interview schedule but also allowing, and even encouraging, the interviewees to elaborate on the particular issues. The interviews took 15–20 minutes on average and were recorded and transcribed.

The interview schedule consisted of two parts. The first line of questioning involved general questions to gain background knowledge and to set the scene. They focused on topics such as the reasons for learning English; attitudes towards English; satisfaction with current level of language proficiency; description of the language classes the person had attended; level of motivation; and the positive/negative factors that affected the learning commitment. The second set of questions concentrated on how the interviewee's motivation changed over the years. We were particularly interested in some prominent motivational ups and downs. The interview was concluded by narrowing the topic further down by 'zooming in' on the interviewees' motivational changes during the past year.

### Data analysis

As described in more detail in Miles and Huberman (1984, 1994) and Crabtree and Miller (1992), the method of analysis employed in this study followed a 'template approach' to data processing. This is a special organizing style of interpretation that uses an analysis guide, or template, as the starting point of the analytical process. We first prepared a template of codes that were relevant to our research questions and then applied them to the actual data. Much of the focus of this interpretation style is on systematically reducing the data so that it can be displayed in an explicit form for interpretation. The grouped extracts corresponding to the various codes were then considered together, and interconnections forming broader patterns were established. We also prepared individual 'time charts' to describe each participant's temporal motivational progression.

## Findings

The following analysis of the dataset will take two directions: the first is aimed at identifying the various motivational factors that were found to influence our subjects throughout their English language learning experience. Although this might sound similar to the standard approach in motivational research, namely to identify motivational factors relevant to the students' learning behaviour, what makes our study different is that, by looking at these factors within the context of the participants' learning history, we could establish increased validity for the identified motives. That is, the list we have obtained was distilled from real-life learning experiences rather than from self-report questionnaires, and therefore the validity of the factors was guaranteed to a certain extent by their salience in the interviewees' personal accounts.

The second direction is aimed at documenting any recurring patterns or themes that resulted in the profound restructuring of the motivational disposition of the language learners, as well as identifying some salient 'motivational transformation episodes'. We consider this direction the main aspect of our investigation and therefore it will be discussed in more detail than the first direction.

### Motivational influences affecting the language learning process

Our initial analysis guide was based on a classification scheme taken from Dörnyei's (2001a, p. 65) summary of the main motivational constructs in the L2 motivational field. We found, however, that the original dimensions listed by Dörnyei were not always sufficiently defined for the purpose of our fine-tuned analysis, and some of the motives found in the dataset did not fit into these categories or overlapped two dimensions. Consequently, we modified this scheme by discarding one dimension ('Macrocontext-Related Dimension') and adding a new dimension to subsume motivational issues related to the 'Host Environment' (which will be explained below). The final seven dimensions that were used are as follows:

1. Affective/Integrative Dimension
2. Instrumental Dimension
3. Self-Concept-Related Dimension
4. Goal-Oriented Dimension
5. Educational-Context-Related Dimension
6. Significant-Other-Related Dimension
7. Host-Environment-Related Dimension

The table in the Appendix lists these dimensions and all their subcategories along with illustrative quotes, also specifying the frequency of the cases when the factors had a positive, negative or neutral impact on the person's motivational development. As can be seen in the table, the observed motivational influences are not equal in terms of the frequency of their occurrence. The highest motivational factor perceived by the subjects to have a *negative* influence was the *Debilitating affective influence* within the Self-Concept-Related Dimension. Each of the interviewees (even those with an overall positive outlook on life) mentioned something related to this subcategory. There were three further motivational factors, mentioned by at least ten interviewees, which had a negative influence on the participants' language learning experience: *Teachers* (15 out of 25), *Satisfaction* (13 out of 25) and *Methodology* (15 out of 25). Of these, *Satisfaction* also belongs to the Self-Concept-Related Dimension, further attesting to the fact that language learning is a highly face-threatening and often negatively loaded emotional experience. The other two factors belong to the Educational-Context-Related

Dimension, and their emergence is in accordance with the potential harmful effect of language teachers and language teaching methodology that has been well documented in studies focusing on *'demotivation'* (for a review, see Dörnyei 2001a, Chapter 7).

The other side of the coin is, luckily, that several motivational factors had a positive effect in our learners' language learning experience. The salience of various instrumental factors was to be expected, given that the target language under investigation was English, the undisputed world language. It was no surprise either that factors belonging to the Affective/Integrative Dimension had more of a positive than a negative impact, given that our sample consisted of fairly motivated learners.

It was reassuring to see that *Teachers* and *Methodology* can also play a beneficial not just a harmful role (as highlighted by 15 and 10 out of 25 participants, respectively). The fact that these two components had a marked impact on both the negative and the positive side underscores the importance of the teacher and the immediate learning situation in the language learning process. The complexity of the role of satisfaction is underscored by the fact that, besides the 13 negative frequencies mentioned, *Satisfaction* was also mentioned 6 times as a positive influence. This, accompanied by the fact that *Confidence* was also mentioned in a positive sense 5 times, indicates that a great deal of further research is needed to find 'recipes' on how to boost the interrelated feelings of satisfaction and confidence, in the spirit of the saying 'success breeds success'.

The emergence of *Goal specificity* underscores the importance of setting concrete learning goals in L2 studies. The origins of some of these goals were found to go way back in the learner's life and they became a reality, or more specified, only as the learners grew older.

Our investigation identified two factors as salient motives that are less frequently mentioned in the L2 literature: *Parental influences* was mentioned 11 times (out of 25), indicating the importance of the home environment. It is interesting that this factor was mentioned only in positive contexts, even though it is common knowledge that parents can influence their children in either way. It may be that more subtle and focused questioning would have revealed less-than-positive effects. *Partner influences* is also a somewhat overlooked motivational component (although, see Campbell 1996). However, common sense suggests, and five occurrences in our dataset confirm this, that the relationships of young adults and adult language learners with a 'significant other' may, directly or indirectly, influence their overall motivational disposition, including their learning experiences, desires and goals.

*Temporal patterns of language learning motivation*

Going through the dataset many times, we could not fail to notice some recurring patterns of motivational change that seemed to be present across varied learning situations. These patterns are related to the motivational factors identified in the previous section, but they appear to be broader in scope and relevance, and result in the profound restructuring of the individual's motivational disposition. They can therefore be seen as *motivational transformation episodes*. Six such salient temporal patterns were identified in the dataset:

1. Maturation and gradually increasing interest
2. Stand-still period
3. Moving into a new life phase
4. Internalizing external goals and 'imported visions'
5. Relationship with a 'significant other'
6. Time spent in the host environment

In the following sections, each of these temporal patterns will be discussed and illustrated individually.

## Maturation and gradually increasing interest (17 out of 25)

Some of the participants in our study mentioned that they had gone through a period in their life – typically some time during their school years and when they started work – in which they felt that they 'matured' or 'gradually became more interested' in learning the English language. They felt they did not understand the significance behind learning English at the beginning of their language studies for a number of reasons: they were too young; they were not aware of what to expect from learning English; it was not their choice; they were not aware of its importance to their future; they thought it was just another school subject; they only learnt it so that they could be distinguished from those who did not know it or just because it was something new. For example:

> I think I was so young that I didn't really realise what it was going to be for me, how important it was going to be. (#20)

However, as they grew older they became more mature and as a result decided that learning English was 'good for them':

> but then, well, I guess it has to do with my age, then I grew up, I start thinking in another way, a mature way, and then I decided that it was good for me. (#19)

Alternatively, they gradually started to become more interested in learning English:

> in the beginning it was not my choice, I must admit it, but then, when the years went by, I started liking it. (#5)

### Stand-still period (9 out of 25)

It seems to be a typical feature of the evolution of L2 motivation that it is not a continuous process. There are sometimes quite considerable stand-still periods in which learners put their language learning motivation on hold because they concentrate on something else. However, when their circumstances change and they again have some free capacity, these learners often re-enter the motivational process at the point where they suspended it. The following two extracts illustrate this well:

> When I finished high school I stopped studying English for several years. The reason was that my degree was in law, I didn't get the chance to choose any subject related to English. During those years, the only contact I had with English was through music. When I finished my degree, I started to learn English again. (#19)

> Well, when I was at university my other lectures were hard and I was focusing on them. So I neglected to continue learning English . . . I neglected it for many years. But after I graduated from university I started learning it again, reading books and learning new words. So all and all I didn't study English for nearly four years. So I had forgot many things I have learned. But then I started again and I remembered. (#2)

### Moving into a new life phase (25 out of 25)

When our subjects entered a new life phase, for example left school and started work, this transition often brought about a change in their learning goals:

> I didn't use my English for several years simply because I didn't need to. In Italy I didn't have many opportunities to speak English and well then I got a new motivation after my degree in the university when I decided to do research and then I needed English and well I had to study English before starting my PhD in law, so I had a new motivation. (#8)

Interestingly, just as people's general life goals often develop gradually throughout the years, we can see a sharpening of the focus in language learning orientations as well. For example, during their early school years many learners wanted to learn English so that they could communicate with others, pass exams, understand songs or movies, or be the teacher's favourite. In later school years goals often became more specific, for example by becoming associated with further studies:

> In high school, my motivation for learning English was to pass the college entrance examination. (#14)

Goals tended to become even more specific when the learner entered university because at this point their whole future career was at stake:

> I really wanted to have some good grades because now it's so difficult to have a job in Portugal so the better your grades are the more your chances are. (#5)

Lastly, goals became even more focused during the 'employment' phase of a person's life. This is a common phase, as illustrated by the following two extracts:

> so when I was seventeen and eighteen, I just learned English at school, but I didn't make any efforts to learn at home . . . when I started working, I realised that I had to learn English to be successful in my job, and to find out what's happening in my area of work. (#24)

> And later on when I started to work, and I had to communicate with people, with my customers, with my colleagues, in the company I work for my motivation changed because of the requirements of the job. (#23)

### Internalizing external goals and 'imported visions' (16 out of 25)

Traditionally, intrinsic and extrinsic motivations have been seen as antagonistic counterparts. However, a shift in self-determination theory suggested that extrinsic motivation could lead to more intrinsic involvement either by the internalization of motives or by discovering new intrinsic aspects of a task through longer engagement in it (Deci and Ryan 1985). This type of temporal pattern also emerged in our dataset: several learners who were originally forced to learn a language became intrinsically interested in it after a while. For example, for some of our subjects English was a compulsory school subject to start with but after a period of time they became more involved in it and started to really enjoy it:

> then because we had to study it so I thought I must learn it well. I started to spend more time on it and gradually I was interested in it. (#1)

33

This internalization process is particularly interesting when it concerns the parents' visions. Some parents more than others play a big role in shaping their children's future. They put an idea into their child's head at an early age and keep reinforcing the idea (e.g., either by talking about it continuously or by doing something like enrolling the child in a private English school) until it becomes internalized by the child by the time he/she has grown up. One of our subjects described this temporal pattern as follows:

> my parents wanted me to study English, you know, it was not really my choice, I didn't come home and say 'oh, now I want to study English', no, it was their choice because they thought at that time that it would be important for my future . . . Yes it was a good choice. Definitely yes, because now I'm studying to be an English teacher, so I guess they chose my career a little bit, you know, because they gave me the opportunity of learning another language at an early age and that influenced my life a lot and now I'm here in England, a thing I would never dream of and in college, in college studying English Studies so yes, it's important. (#10)

### Relationship with a 'significant other' (5 out of 25)

As was already discussed in the previous section, partners played an important role in the learning development of some of our subjects:

> My girlfriend moved to England for half a year, and this of course was a big motivation to speak English better, if you wanted to visit her, or things like that, I naturally had to come in contact with many English-speaking people. (#24)

The ultimate motivational force in this respect was forming a relationship with a native speaker of the target language:

> I have an English girlfriend now, and things are going very good. I hope very much to settle here. (#9)

### Time spent in the host environment (14 out of 25)

With the increase in international travel and communication, spending some time in the host environment is becoming a realistic possibility for a growing number of language learners. Our data suggest that this experience can have a significant motivational impact, both in the positive and the negative sense. Sometimes a holiday, a short visit or attending an international school in an English-speaking country can boost the learner's confidence and motivation:

> Yes, positive my travel to Ireland. I enjoyed it very much, I learnt
> very much and when I came back to Spain I was looking for
> everything written in English, like magazines, books, and
> everything filmed in English. I was very interested in English. (#16)

Interestingly, in a recent study using an autobiographical approach, Lim (2002) also highlights the significant motivating potential of a trip to the host environment (in her case, Australia). Her account is an excellent illustration of the fact that a *motivational transformational episode* constitutes more than a mere increase in motivation; it restructures the learner's motivational disposition, putting it on a new, often fast, track:

> This trip [to Australia] changed my perceptions about learning a
> foreign language. I was very surprised by the fact that I didn't have
> much trouble travelling by myself for a month. I could speak with
> other English speakers and made friends with no problem. I
> started to believe that my English must not be so bad and I didn't
> have to produce perfect pronunciation and sentences to be
> understood. Because I no longer believed that perfection was
> necessary to communicate and because I had shown that I could
> communicate, I now regained control over my own learning. . . .
> That experience – managing with my English – gave me great
> inspiration and motivation to continue to improve. I discovered
> that what my teachers had been telling me was not true. I could
> reach my goal without being perfect.
>
> (Lim 2002, p. 100)

On the other hand, putting one's L2 proficiency to the test in real encounters can also turn out to be a demotivating experience if the learners realize that the L2 tuition in their home countries has not prepared them sufficiently for communication with native speakers and for coping with the everyday needs of living in the host country.

> But in fact, when I looked at my level of English I could realize
> that my English was not so good as I thought. So my motivation
> decreased. (#19)

## Conclusion

The purpose of this exploratory study was to identify and document the different motivational influences and temporal patterns that seemed to play a role in our participants' language learning development over an extended period. Our findings support arguments in the literature (cf. Dörnyei 2001a) that motivation is not a stable state but a dynamic process that fluctuates over time. In our participants' accounts we found a variety of factors that had either a negative or a positive impact on their motivational disposition. During the second phase of the analysis, we identified several salient 'motivational transformation episodes', which were more general in their scope than the various motivational influences found earlier. Although these findings are admittedly preliminary, they confirm our belief that adopting a process-oriented perspective is a particularly promising future direction for motivation research.

Within a process-oriented approach, the analysis of long-term motivational moves and shifts is a central issue, and therefore this approach lends itself to biographical/autobiographical research. We have found that learning histories can shed new light on the L2 motivational complex by presenting the various motives that are normally considered in isolation in a contextualized and interrelated manner. In addition, the contextual information concerns both the environmental and the temporal context, thereby offering a genuinely 'rich description'. Finally, there is a further layer of biographical/autobiographical data that is unique: the emphasis and value that the informant inherently assigns to the various episodes by placing them in the whole life sequence and outlining their consequences and corollaries. As we have argued before, the validity of this attached value is guaranteed to a certain extent by the salience of the particular episode within the interviewee's personal account. In sum, taking a biographical/autobiographical approach has been a surprisingly positive and fruitful experience – we hope that the current study, as well as the other contributions in this volume, will inspire further research along these lines.

# Appendix

List of the motivational factors identified in the study, with frequency counts and illustrative examples.

| Dimension | Frequency of positive influences | Frequency of negative influences | Frequency of neutral influences | Illustrations |
|---|---|---|---|---|
| *Affective/Integrative Dimension* | | | | |
| • Attitudes towards the target language | 11 | — | — | I like English because ab it's not so complex. I mean for lay people to start English it's a little bit easier than to start Russian because the grammar is not so complex and also the pronunciation, I like the English pronunciation very much. And the way of speaking, I think that I . . . more than love this language, I adore it. (#6) |
| • Attitudes towards language learning | 9 | 2 | — | Yes, I enjoyed learning English when I was in primary school because I got good marks at that time. But I thought English was very interesting at that time and because it was a fresh thing you know and I liked interesting and fresh things. (#15) |
| • Attitudes towards the target community | 10 | 5 | — | Interviewer: Have you ever thought of giving up? Participant: Learning English? Never, never! I am learning lots of things and . . . it's not only about the language, it's also about the culture . . . (#20) |
| • Mood | 5 | 5 | — | It depends firstly on the mood of the person, sometimes we don't feel that motivated, that is something to do with your inside, your feelings. (#10) |

Appendix (cont.)

| Dimension | Frequency of positive influences | Frequency of negative influences | Frequency of neutral influences | Illustrations |
|---|---|---|---|---|
| *Instrumental Dimension* | | | | |
| • Current job | 7 | — | — | When I started to work, I realized that I had to learn English to be successful in my job and to find out what is happening in my line of work (#24) |
| • Desired job | 15 | — | — | You have to learn it because your future career as a lawyer, ab will depend mostly on a person's knowledge of English. (#14) |
| • Colleagues | 1 | — | — | another thing that motivated me is that many of my colleagues that I got to know recently come maybe from Slovenia or Italy, and English is the only language I can communicate in with them. (#24) |
| • Further study | 13 | 3 | — | to me it was important to study English, as that would help me pass the university exams . . . (#12) |
| • English as a lingua franca | 12 | — | — | if you can speak English, you can communicate with people all over the world almost (#17) |
| • English is part of the image of a modern person | 1 | — | — | I believe that nowadays being able to speak at least one foreign language especially English is essential. (#12) |
| *Self-Concept-Related Dimension* | | | | |
| • Confidence | 5 | — | — | Well, I think that mainly ups, because I feel more confident speaking English than I was before, because I almost always practice at school. (#25) |
| • Satisfaction | 6 | 13 | — | I am so disappointed with my English! I have studied English for so many years and I still can't speak it freely or fluently. (#5) |

| Category | | | | Quote |
|---|---|---|---|---|
| • Acceptance of one's limits | 6 | 1 | 1 | *I've got a limit, I can't go beyond it. I will never be a native speaker and I don't even want other people to expect that I'm perfect in English . . . (#18)* |
| • Debilitating factors | — | 25 | — | *Last year I applied for a scholarship and I thought that I gave them a very good application . . . but unfortunately I didn't pass, and after that time I had a soul search and my motivation to learn . . . weakened for a while because of this unlucky situation. (#6)* |
| • Self-determination (own decision to learn English) | 2 | — | — | *When I finished my degree it was a personal decision to start learning English again, so it made me more interested to learn English than I was before . . . (#19)* |
| *Goal-Oriented Dimension* | | | | |
| • Mastery orientation (learning for knowing) | 4 | — | — | *Yes, because if we are motivated and if we really like that subject we will look for more information about it. If we're not, we'll just write the exam and then, never talk about that subject again. (#5)* |
| • Performance orientation – Demonstrating ability | 4 | — | — | *There are many aspects of motivation. I mean many factors that affect my motivation. But the main factor is to be successful in the coursework that I do here and to communicate with people easily and to be characterized as a person that knows a foreign language very well. (#2)* |
| – Getting good grades | 8 | — | — | *Interviewer: Ok, so what motivated you then, being in this kind of class, what motivated you to continue to study?* <br> *Participant: To have high marks! (#22)* |
| – Outdoing other students | 3 | — | — | *We are in a group in which almost all the students were interested in English. So there was a big competition between us. (#11)* |
| • Goal specificity | 12 | — | — | *And why I started the learning of English? – I mean, I think that a person who had uh goal uh–has to have first of all a very . . . precise goal . . . (#6)* |

Appendix (*cont.*)

| Dimension | Frequency of positive influences | Frequency of negative influences | Frequency of neutral influences | Illustrations |
|---|---|---|---|---|
| *Educational-Context-Related Dimension* | | | | |
| • Teacher | 15 | 15 | — | *Since the beginning I liked it and when I was in high school I started enjoying it a little bit more because of a teacher I had, she was really, ah, a role model for me you know, the way she, she taught us, it was really good and that made me love this language even more and that made me understand that 'OK, now I want to be an English teacher.' (#10)* |
| • Fellow students/classmates | 2 | 4 | — | *Well, if the group I'm in is composed of people I dislike then I won't feel motivated towards that class . . . Yeah in my first year it was, apart from being a big class, it was full of people that I didn't know and people that I didn't consider nice. (#5)* |
| • Curriculum | 3 | — | — | *And another main difficulty I can think of is the educational system. Maybe you don't think it's very serious, but I think it is. When we were in high school, we were taught English in order to take exams, to pass the entrance exam of high school and university . . . So, I think the direction of our education system is not correct. (#23)* |
| • Methodology | 10 | 15 | — | *The classes were a little bit boring because the teacher didn't give us the opportunity to participate in class. He explained the grammar and the vocabulary, but we couldn't speak in class or listen to native speakers. (#19)* |
| • English as a compulsory subject | 1 | 1 | 14 | *I learned it actually because I had to learn it in school, so this was my initial motivation, just, I did it because I had to do it. (#24)* |

| | | | | |
|---|---|---|---|---|
| • Class size | — | 3 | 2 | Our classes in Portugal are too crowded. There are a lot of people in the same class. So I think it's not really motivating. (#5) |
| *Significant-Other-Related Dimension* | | | | |
| • Parents | 10 | — | 1 | Well, I started when I was just five years old, and the main reason was because my parents thought it was going to be interesting to start learning a new language, and I was really, really young, and they thought it was easier to do it then. (#20) |
| • Family | 4 | — | — | I see my brother here, first because he speaks good English and second he has a life here. So I think maybe I can do the same. (#9) |
| • Friends | 4 | 3 | — | I made a lot of friends during that year. I lived with another family, my host family. I am still in contact with them now, even though it has been three years ago and I call my friends, I write to them so that is obviously a big motivation. (#1) |
| • Partner | 4 | 1 | — | My girlfriend moved to England for half a year, and this of course was a big motivation to speak English better, if you wanted to visit her, or things like that . . . (#24) |
| *Host-Environment-Related Dimension* | | | | |
| • L2 contact | 8 | 3 | — | But here I'm talking from when I wake up till I go to bed. I talk with everybody and then I go to classes and I listen to the teachers and I listen to everybody who is speaking, you know, to improve my accent and this is really good, it's really interesting. (#10) |
| • Inability to integrate | 1 | 7 | — | Little, very little because I have not got so many English friends here or can't find friends. Because I live with my friends, my Turkish friends, so we always speak to each other in Turkish. So it is very bad to live with people from your own nationality. (#2) |
| • Length of stay | 2 | — | — | If I stay here for long time, ten years, I can speak like a native speaker . . . (#4) |

# 4 Emotion processes in second language acquisition

*Sufumi So with Rocío Domínguez*

This project began rather casually. In Fall 1998 Rocío Domínguez (the second author), a Peruvian Spanish–German bilingual, was admitted to the doctoral programme in Second Language Acquisition (SLA) at Carnegie Mellon University in Pittsburgh, USA, where I had recently been hired as assistant professor of SLA. Rocío enrolled in my course 'Introduction to Second Language Acquisition' in that semester. One day she was in my office and somehow our conversation turned to her ongoing process of English language learning. The story she told me that day was vivid and enlightening and made me want to learn more about her experience of learning English as a third language. Rocío agreed to meet with me regularly for the next couple of months, simply recounting her recent experience related to her acquisition of the English language. I remained a listener, occasionally asking questions for clarification and further detail. We met six times in total for this purpose for about an hour each time between 28 October 1998 and 8 February 1999. Like the day of our first session, the day for the last session had not been pre-planned. When we both felt we had seen sufficient number of 'interesting' things in Rocío's stories, we were eager to switch our dialogist hat to that of the researcher. Each of our conversations was tape recorded in its entirety and later transcribed verbatim by Rocío. I then checked the transcriptions for accuracy as I listened to the tapes.

## Theoretical orientation

In brief, theoretical backdrops evident in this paper are the notion of emergentism on the one hand and the view of human action – internal and external – as mediated action on the other. In retrospect, other than my desire to learn about the language learner's experience first hand, I was experimenting with the emergentist approach to knowledge building (Sawyer 2002) in this project. As such, I was focusing on 'experience' as a method and an object of research. John Dewey (1938/1963, pp. 43–4) stated:

> An experience is always what it is because of a transaction taking place between an individual and what, at the time, constitutes his

> environment . . . The environment, in other words, is whatever
> conditions interact with personal needs, desires, purposes, and
> capacities to create the experience which is had.

Research and interpretive processes in this project emerged simultaneously from our active engagement within different systems and at different levels of analysis. My orientation as to the empirical mechanics of such emergent processes in the present work is to view Rocío's language learning experience as mediated action (e.g., Wertsch 1991, 1998) and examine the properties of her experience emerging from the interaction of organism (individual psychology) and environment. In particular I will focus on 'emotion processes' (Sherer 2000) in Rocío's experience because that is what stood out in the transcripts.

When patterns in Rocío's emotions and English acquisition began to emerge in my mind, I searched for a theoretical frame that could guide us in the analysis and interpretation of the data. The framework should capture the essence of what emotion *is*. Emotion, as we were beginning to see in Rocío's episodes, is the psychological outcome of dynamic interactions between different layers of internal and external systems – physiological, cognitive, behavioural and social. Ongoing conditions surrounding Rocío affected at once the way she felt inside and the way she saw the state of her English acquisition and her surroundings. This moment-to-moment, subtle and complex interaction of the inner and the outer side of Rocío's self seemed to amplify or disintegrate the flow of her emotion processes, with greater energy leading to a higher degree of systemic organization. The whole system appears to have followed a globally predictable, yet locally unpredictable, path. This phenomenon, I thought, would be best captured with the emergentist approach, which holds that 'nothing exists except the component parts and their interactions' and that 'phenomena are complex systems in which more complex and differentiated "higher level" structures emerge from the organization and interaction of simpler, "lower level" component parts' (Sawyer 2002, p. 4).

When Rocío's emotional experience is viewed from this emergentist perspective, it makes sense to take mediated action as a unit of analysis. This means, according to Wertsch (1998), that the focus of the research is neither solely on the individual nor solely on the environment. It rather formulates its stance vis-à-vis this antinomy between individual and environment; it is about the dialectic between agent and situation. Human action – that is, mental action in the case of the present study – is seen as a synchronized mechanism of the internal and the external.

## Emotions and SLA

The successful management of one's emotions, or affective factors such as motivation, anxiety, empathy and self-esteem, can lead to successful learning. This idea sounds commonplace today as the works of Gardner (e.g., 1983, 2000), Sternberg (1985, 1988), and Goleman (1995), which provide a much more expanded and balanced view of intelligence than the traditional notion of IQ advanced by Alfred Binet early in the twentieth century (Binet and Simon, 1973), continue to arouse popular interest.

Since the early stage of the development of SLA as a field of study, research on the learner's internal factors in relation to learning success has been a major area of interest. Book-length treatments of the issues include Gardner and Lambert (1972) on attitude and motivation, Horwitz and Young (1991) on anxiety, Ehrman and Oxford (1995) on cognition, personality and feelings, Schumann (1997) on emotions, and Arnold (1999) on affective factors and SLA. Earlier studies relied solely on batteries of self-check tests of affective variables and statistical analyses to distinguish more significant from less significant psychological variables in SLA. More recent work, complementing the earlier work that sought to discover general trends, focuses on individual learners' experiences so as to address the common phenomenon of variable success in SLA through the use of open-ended and semi-structured interviews (Ehrman 1996), and diaries and autobiographies (Schumann 1997). These qualitative approaches to the study of language learners' emotions should be recognized as appropriate research strategies in building more ecologically valid models of the emotion process in real-life and concrete situational settings. Further, emotion is constantly generated, unfolded, and changed through multiple recursive effects at any one moment. This fluidity of emotion – a complex, multifaceted psychological phenomenon – may be better captured by examining the quality of people's subjective experiences.

My work with Rocío is thus situated in the qualitative tradition of inquiry known as interpretive biographical study (Denzin 1989) and aims to understand how her emotion regulatory processes influenced the course of the emotion trajectory in regard to her acquisition of English. The focus has been on gathering stories, identifying stories that indicate pivotal events, exploring their meanings, and providing an interpretation for the experience recounted in the form of stories. In describing Rocío's emotional experience, I shall focus on the psychological moments of her mental action and formulate psychological claims in such a way that their relation to context is always apparent. First, however, her background is introduced in her own voice below.

44

## Rocío's story[1]

I was born and raised in Lima, Peru. My mother tongue is Spanish but I attended a German school in Peru, where I started learning German at the age of six. When I was 13 years old, I went to Germany to study for three months. I did the same in the following year when I was 14. I adapted very easily to German culture and made many German friends while I was in Germany. I remember I was able to think in German even after my return to Peru and I was very proud of my native-like German accent. The common notion of *Deutsche Sprache schwere Sprache* [German is tough to learn] was never true for me. This experience of my first foreign-language learning made me believe that I had the special ability to learn languages.

Despite the advice given to me, I did not take any English language courses during high school. I was simply not interested in learning a foreign language as a school subject. Upon entering college, however, I realized that I had to read a lot in English because most of the course readings were written in English. Even though I did not have much trouble with reading or listening to English, I enrolled in English language classes anyway for one year and a half. English grammar was very easy compared to German. In English classes, however, I began noticing that I could not pronounce English words as the teacher did. I found myself confused and frustrated. Whenever I tried to speak English, German words came out of my mouth. I had no problem with English grammar, yet I could not pronounce English words. I was disappointed at my oral performance in English and stopped taking English classes. Besides, I was able to read English texts without difficulty, which was sufficient for me to do well in college courses in Peru.

When I was admitted to a graduate programme in the USA, I worried about many things despite my previous experience of studying abroad. I was concerned about going away from my home country and having to stay alone in a new environment. But my biggest fear was English, the fact that I would have to function in English for schoolwork and day-to-day chores. I was scared but I was also thinking, before my departure to the USA, that I should be all right once I got there. I was wrong. It was overwhelming just to set up my daily routine in this new place. Having to arrange almost everything by phone was a nightmare. People spoke very fast. I was too ashamed to ask them to speak again or slowly. I tried to avoid speaking on the phone as much as I could.

Soon my first semester as a graduate student in the USA began. The problem with English loomed large on the academic side of my life as well. I was expected to speak up and express my views in class. I felt inferior and I was increasingly uncomfortable with what I came to be. The more stressed I was, the worse I performed in English. I had never been shy in my life, but I definitely became so in English. My problems with English were many. I mixed up the present and past tenses. I did not have a large vocabulary to express myself. I could not connect sentences well. German words and sentences kept popping up from my mouth when I tried to speak English. I did not know what to do. I was feeling lost and pessimistic. That's when I began sharing my ongoing experiences of learning English with Sufumi.

## Emotion processes of Rocío's English language acquisition

Understandably Rocío's account of her initial days in Pittsburgh is filled with such words as *afraid*, *hard*, *worried*, *fear* and *stress*.

> When I came here, I was very worried because I haven't speak English at all but with a few times and I tried to make good sentences. I tried to produce grammaticality good sentences. It was very very hard. I had a lot of stress. And I already also found myself not very fluent and that bothered me.[2]

Upon her arrival Rocío first stayed with an American English–Spanish bilingual, Anne,[3] and Anne's English-monolingual partner, John.

> When I came here the first two weeks I was hiding at Anne's house so I really I was very very afraid and I came to the university for the orientation and then after six o'clock I run, stayed home. I didn't went out unless I went with Anne or John. . . . I try to speak in Spanish with Anne and try to avoid to speak with John and I try to avoid speaking by phone. I don't like speaking by phone because I can't get what people was saying to me.

Rocío's main concerns with English were grammar, pronunciation and sociolinguistic rules. She described her way of dealing with English in those early days as 'avoidance, avoid, avoid everything I can't do right'.

On the one hand, she tried to cling to her native language, Spanish, in which she felt most comfortable. She preferred to go out with her Spanish-speaking friends and she chose to live with Spanish-speaking housemates so that she could speak her mother tongue at home. On the other hand, her non-fluent English continued to bother her and she was keenly aware of the importance of improving her English. To do so, however, she first needed to deal with her negative emotions.

> I recognized I have to be a little bit less demanding so and I recognized that it's going to take time to pick up the language, pick up the use. So I started not to bother for such things and try to find ways to practicing English. . . . With Machiko and Emi

[*Rocío's fellow students in the same graduate programme who are native speakers of Japanese*], for example, I try to spend a lot of time to speaking English and also with Joy [*another fellow student of Rocío who is a native speaker of English*], she speaks very good Spanish but I try to speak English with her and I make a lot of question and everybody there [*in the graduate students' office*] hate me because I always ask English question, daily questions like 'How do you say if have a hole in your socking [*she meant* 'stocking']?' and 'How do you say when you dress up or off?' [*laughing*]

By this time she had been in the USA for three to four weeks. Rocío realized that her fellow students, who were also non-native speakers of English, did not know proper English expressions for these despite the fact that they had been living in the USA for a couple of years. She said, 'They are having troubles like me [*laughing*].' She also noticed that many of her Hispanic friends 'don't care about their [foreign] accent [in speaking English]. They don't care about their mistakes or their errors.' And she came to the conclusion that 'second [language] learner make mistakes' and that there is nothing to be ashamed of in it.

Some people have a very hard accent and they don't care about it. And I found my accent not so hard . . . I found that if they don't care their accent, why should I have trouble with this? So and I heard so many people in restaurants, library, store, speak in English in so many weird things, so many weird ways. Who cares about it?

Shortly after this realization (i.e., about six weeks after her arrival in the USA), Rocío was put in a situation where she was compelled to communicate in English, oftentimes on the phone, with shop attendants, staff at gas, electricity and telephone companies, and the like to set up her life and that of her Hispanic housemates, one of whom spoke little English.

Rita [*Rocío's musician housemate, who was new to the USA, and spoke very little English*] and I went together to the supermarket. We went together to Goodwill. We went together everywhere. But I . . . I speak. I'm the one who speak. She doesn't speak at all. Or if she received any phone call, I have to translate for her. She also want to me to call people to get some jobs. So I call people. I don't know a word about music. I don't know about this stuff. But okay, I'm going to do this because she need the money.

Rocío saw in Rita her own fear of speaking English.

She had the same concerns than me. She was very afraid to speak by phone . . . and she choose me to do this work to speak by phone to do everything . . . I tried to calm her every time. I . . . I

47

> . . . find that I can do this. So okay I'm going to do her work. I'm going to be a little bit protective for her . . .

This situation eventually led Rocío to overcome her own fear of speaking English.

> since I found this girl [*Rita*] I somehow my own fears were gone because I have her fears to take care and help . . . somehow my own fears disappear by doing this. I'm not doing this for me. I'm doing this for other. I'm trying to help other so and I . . . I wasn't anxious by speaking for other. So I started by speaking phone, speaking by phone . . . I'm speaking for Rita. I'm going to translate her and I was, no, I wasn't worried to speak wrong, not at all because it's not for me. I don't know how to explain this. It was very very odd.

While she was still much concerned about her 'many troubles with type of verbs and prepositions', Rocío began enjoying impromptu English study sessions with her native and non-native English-speaking peers at school.

> I'm having a lot of fun doing this. I found that I can have fun doing this instead of being anxious or being nervous or being afraid to make mistakes. So mistakes are good because by making mistakes I'm going to learn.

Alongside these psychological changes about the use of English, Rocío was becoming increasingly comfortable with her new environment in a foreign land and ready to embrace the diversity, open-mindedness and freedom afforded by her new surroundings.

> I find here more comfortable with this relativistic perspective . . . it is very comfortable because I am used to a very narrow perspective of life. You have to do this, this, and this. You can't do this and this because there is no way. There are not so many people, different people . . . If you came here and you see a variety of people, you are more comfortable because, okay, this is my way of doing things and respect the others. People are going to respect mine . . . [Here] people are different, people are different, a way of life. Nobody cares what you wear. Nobody cares what you do and it is, it is I feel comfortable because I know I'm out of my country, out of my home, out of my way of do things. So I don't have any strait [*she meant* 'strict'] rules to follow. A little bit free to choose whatever I want to do and that's a relief.

Clearly, Rocío now felt accepted for who she was in the USA She once said, 'Nobody said, "No, you are not speaking good." I haven't had any bad experience at all here with being a Hispanic and that's one thing afraid of, to be discriminated.'

Rocío's problems with English syntax, pronunciation and pragmatics persisted. She also began noticing her code-mixing Spanish, German and English words after being in the USA and struggling with the English language for ten weeks or so. Another type of problem she began to encounter around this time was negative transfer from one language to another, interestingly oftentimes from English to Spanish (i.e., literal translation of English phrases to Spanish). Rocío related episodes of these language problems using such words as *nasty, weird, upsetting, annoying, confusing, unhappy,* and *awful* – expressions of frustration. She was also frustrated to find herself 'being shy in English only because I don't know the language, . . . because I'm afraid of people say "she is not a native speaker"'. Concurrently she was steadily developing confidence in her English as indicated in the following accounts:

[Account 1] I am feeling now that I'm not anxious any more because of making myself clear in English. And also found that the quiet, the more relax I am, the better I speak.

[Account 2] I was on the bus on my way here and there were two, there were a couple. It was having a conversation. And didn't pay attention to this. But I, any point, I realized that I understand what they're saying without paying attention. I was thinking in other things . . . and suddenly I realize that I was understanding and almost following the conversation, but not because I really wanted but because it wasn't a noise at all. It was no more a noise.

[Account 3] We saw a movie and I realize that I wasn't paying attention at the language. I was paying attention at the, at the, what was going in the movie. I was wondering what is going to happen next, who is the bad guy? and so on. I wasn't paying attention at what they were saying . . . then I realize I was understanding. So that's why I haven't paid much attention to this. I didn't, I didn't need to do this.

[Account 4] This semester [*Rocío's second semester*] I really don't care. I mean when I want speak [in class], I raise my hand as I used to do when I was a student home. . . . so I don't care about [*inaudible*] something very very grammatical correct. That's not the point. The point is to express and to contribute and to have some feedback, yeah, to share something with other people.

These experiences brought Rocío positive emotions about English language learning as she herself noted:

That's good news, yeah, is sort of lower stress. I don't have to make an extra effort. I wasn't feeling that I was doing this extra effort but actually I feel the difference. Now I feel a little bit relief than before.

Gradually her pessimism over English acquisition was replaced by optimism. At the same time she was, in a way, becoming more realistic.

> Even [though it may be] tough I really know that I'm going to be able to improve it [*my English*] a lot. And [before] I was afraid I'm not going to, I thought the obstacles are going to be too much or too big to do this. Now I'm sure that it is not going to be perfect but it has not to be [*she meant* 'need not be'] perfect. So it is going to be okay and maybe it's like a little bit, I feel a little bit more secure about this . . . My goal is try to improve speaking as well as I can, that, knowing that certain there is a limit because of my age probably and because of my background of other languages . . . My perception is not that I'm speaking better but that I don't care, I mean, I really want to properly acquired English but I already I finally realized that I need time. So I'm not anxious about the idea 'when I'm going to speak good or not.' That's not the question. Now the when is not the question. The question is, okay it needs time. When it comes, it comes. I'm going to know it. I'm going to feel it. I'm going to experience this. So this is a very important factor because I am, now I know I make a lot of mistakes. That's not the issue. So I realized that making mistakes is part of acquiring language.

By December Rocío came to terms with the process of her English acquisition.

> I made my decision. So, okay, things are good. I think I can do this [*graduate work*]. I'm going to stay [in the USA] . . . This is very much related with language, I think. I'm comfortable with the language, with my acquisition of the language . . . Also my acquisition the cultural differences, I was, I thought it is going to be too tough. Then I realized it was a little bit tough but not impossible to reach. So I show myself that I can make it.

She also realized that she was wrong to expect the same process and results of her German acquisition that had begun at her young age and under different conditions. As her level of comfort with the English language increased, she became more comfortable about being a trilingual – 'I'm realizing since I'm comfortable with the three of them [*Spanish, German, and English*], so I can choose whatever I want to express myself.' Further, she said:

> I'm not longer have this attitude 'I have to speak a [*she meant* 'only one'] language' because that's not the way it is in my mind. So I don't have one here [*pointing to her head*], I have many [languages] . . . When I really relax about this, when I don't care, then I started to feel better, comfortable and try to see, 'Okay, I have my own way to say things.'

Rocío's developing sense of identity became clear during these first couple of months of intense experience with a new language and a new culture.

> I don't feel like I'm abandon something important like identity. It's about performing, so can communicate fluent with other people . . . If I'm going to be here for a while, why should I resist? What do I gain by resistance? It is going to be worse so but still I don't feel like I'm losing something . . . I have my own [Hispanic, and more specifically Peruvian] culture. It doesn't mean that I don't want American culture. It means that I have my own. So I don't need to feel like part of this community. I have my small community. And it's healthy to realize that I have my own identity. I'm not going to be an American. I don't want to be an American. It's impossible.

Finally she said, referring to her habit of code-mixing, 'Before it was not clear. Now I'm a little bit more self-conscious about what I'm doing probably because I accept what I'm doing. I'm trying to see it as a fact. So I start feeling relief.'

## Discussion

In his recent book introducing the research literature on SLA, Scovel (2001) states:

> [O]f all the SLA variables discussed in this book, emotions are the ones we are still struggling to come to grips with. The great irony is that they could very well end up being the most influential force in language acquisition, but SLA researchers have not even come close to demonstrating such a claim. . . . More than any other topic covered in this book, affective variables are the area that SLA researchers understand the least. (p. 140)

Scovel's remark can be read as signalling the need for a radical departure from such classic paradigms as experimental and correlational approaches to research on emotion and language acquisition. The new paradigm should emphasize *emotion process* (rather than *emotional state*), that is, dynamic self-organizing processes of emotions that are non-linear and constantly emerging through the causal interdependence among internal and external variables on different timescales. I hope my discussion of Rocío's emotion episodes with which her narrative is charged can yield insight into the emotion processes in SLA.

My discussion is centred on one specific question, following the tradition of the study of emotional intelligence (i.e., the study that considers the place of emotion processes in intelligent behaviour): how are emotions responded to and regulated? Emotions are fluid and emergent phenomena that result from the interplay of implicit and explicit mental processes. Emotions can be generated, responded to and regulated in better or worse ways, and the ways in which individuals go about emotion regulation can shape the success of their undertakings. My main task in this section is to evaluate Rocío's ability to function optimally in her varying life circumstances as they unfolded over time. I shall do so by carefully examining the processes of her automatic responses to and deliberate control of emotions revealed in her narrative.

Over the period of the first few months after her arrival in the USA, various kinds of emotions were aroused in Rocío in relation to her English language acquisition and they shifted corresponding to her experiences and circumstances. Emotional responses emerged and the processes that produced and modified their trajectories ensued. It is in these processes that I believe one of the keys to successful accomplishment of one's undertaking lies. The question is whether one is capable of recognizing and regulating emotion in an efficient and productive manner and thus of dealing with the environment effectively.

To organize the potentially innumerable emotion regulatory processes, Gross (1998) proposed five conceptual categories: situation selection, situation modification, attention deployment, cognitive change and response modulation. All these five forms of emotion regulation can be identified in Rocío's episodes and they occurred at different points – more or less in this order – in the overall process of emotion generation and regulation over the period studied. Negative emotions, which were aroused in the face of the totally English-speaking environment in her early days in the USA, were responded to by simply avoiding the situations where she had to communicate in English. This form of emotion regulation, according to Gross's categorization, is situation selection. Gradually she began making active efforts to modify the situation directly so as to alter its emotional impact. She sought out a peer group who spoke her mother tongue to socialize in the language she felt most comfortable with. At the same time she looked for opportunities to improve her English so as to satisfy the felt need. By engaging in these kinds of emotion regulatory acts – known as situation modification – Rocío tried to change the ongoing social environment and brought a new situation into existence. Instances of attention deployment are where Rocío ruminated on her feelings and their consequences. The following utterance illustrates this strategy well: 'I recognized I have to be a little bit less demanding so and I recognized that it's going to take time to pick up the language, pick up the use. So I started not to bother for such things and try to find ways to practicing English.'

The next category of emotion regulatory strategies is called cognitive change. Downward social comparison and cognitive reframing were the cognitive-change strategies Rocío often used to manage the perceived situation as her days in the USA moved on. For downward social comparison, she would compare her performance in English with that of other non-native speakers (i.e., her fellow Japanese students and Hispanic friends), which she found was no better than hers, thereby altering her construal of her English proficiency and decreasing negative emotion. An example of cognitive reframing is that when Rocío began helping her Hispanic housemate with little English proficiency, she noticed that her fear of speaking English, especially of speaking on the phone, was gone and she began focusing on communication rather than production of grammatical sentences. Another good example of cognitive reframing concerns her code-mixing. Rocío experienced *failure* with respect to the goal of expressing herself entirely in English. Later, however, she reframed it as something positive with regard to another goal of being a multilingual.

Permeable boundaries among emotion regulation strategies are particularly evident in cognitive-change and response-modulation strategies observed in Rocío's emotion episodes. Response modulation, the last category of Gross's system, refers to influencing emotional response tendencies. Rocío tried constantly to reevaluate the state of her English acquisition cognitively (cognitive change) so as to induce more positive emotional responses (response modulation). This is most evident in her remark that begins with 'Even [though it may be] tough I really know that I'm going to be able to improve it a lot.' In the same quote she reasoned out answers that might explain her current state of English proficiency and came up with a solution for dealing with emotions over the progress of her English acquisition: to reaffirm her goal, recognize the fact that she is in the *process* of learning, and appreciate English learning for its own sake.

These observations attest to Rocío's intelligent management of emotions. She seems capable not only of identifying and differentiating emotion experiences but also of knowing how to invoke emotion regulatory processes in order to move ahead in the direction of achieving a goal. It appears that Rocío possesses a large repertoire of emotion regulatory strategies, thereby producing a flexible behavioural repertoire to deal with various emotions generated by her internal and external situations. How might her emotional intelligence have facilitated the process of her English acquisition? To touch on this question, I shall relate briefly what became of Rocío's English proficiency afterwards.

After successfully completing the first year of graduate study at Carnegie Mellon University, during the first part of which the present study was carried out, Rocío continued her study in the programme. Her

English proficiency has since improved quite visibly. Her competence in English is now proven by the successful completion of her master's thesis and a number of conference presentations in English. Her doctoral dissertation, of course written in English, is also now near completion. The present study provides no hard evidence as to the presence or absence of causal relationships between emotional intelligence and SLA. However, considering the widely recognized role that emotions play in learning, it is not unreasonable to think that Rocío's progress in English acquisition was facilitated by her emotional intelligence, that is, the ways she managed her emotions effectively[4] so as to achieve a given goal.

## Conclusion

In this paper I have spelt out what Rocío did when she tried to regulate emotions as they were generated in the process of acquiring English. Her emotion regulatory processes were characterized based on Gross's process model of emotion response tendencies and the five major points suggested by the model were identified at which she influenced the course of the emotion trajectory as regards to her acquisition of English. Rocío, who appeared as an emotionally intelligent individual in the present study, seemed to know how to manage emotions flexibly in such a way that is well suited to a given situation in the face of constantly fluctuating and competing demands from within and outside.

Recently the role of emotions has been much discussed in everyday life (e.g., Goleman 1995), in education in general (e.g., Gardner 2000), and more specifically in foreign language learning (e.g., Arnold 1999). Clearly, questions about how emotions can or should be managed in order to optimize one's learning are a worthwhile domain for serious investigation of SLA researchers. A particularly fertile land of inquiry seems to lie beneath the question of how cooperation between reason and emotion can be achieved so as to motivate and sustain action directed towards long-term objectives. When such inquiry is carried out taking a process perspective and paying attention to individual differences, I believe, our understanding of the role of emotions in SLA will improve substantially.

## Notes

1. A few months after the completion of our conversations Rocío was asked to write a narrative of her background and previous language-related experiences. The text presented here is minimally edited for readability.

2. Quotes from the transcripts are given without fillers such as *um, uh, well,* and *you know* for readability. Grammatical errors are, however, left uncorrected so as to give the reader a sense of the proficiency level Rocío possessed in spoken English at the time of this study. Other conventions used in transcription are: (a) . . . for utterances that are omitted for brevity, (b) [*italics*] for explanatory remarks and (c) [words] for words that are added to enhance the clarity of quoted utterances.

3. This and other personal names that appear in this paper are pseudonyms.

4. Here I shall hasten to add that this 'effectiveness' is only my subjective judgement as observer. Rocío's emotional intelligence was not measured using such existing (reportedly reliable but not necessarily valid) tests as Multifactor Emotional Intelligence Scale (MEIS), Mayer-Salovey-Caruso Emotional Intelligence Test (MSCEIT), Levels of Emotional Awareness Scale (LEAS), Bar-On Emotional Quotient Inventory (EQ-I), Trait Meta-Mood Scale (TMMS) and Shutte Self-Report Inventory (SSRI) (Ciarrochi *et al.* 2001). It would be interesting to see how Rocío might fare in any of these 'objective' measures of emotional intelligence and how well her level of emotional intelligence might predict the level of her success in language acquisition.

# 5   Is there language acquisition after 40? Older learners speak up

*Lois Bellingham*

As the learning of languages expands across our world, and nations and cultures are forced into ever closer and more frequent communication, we see adults of all ages attempting to acquire a new language. They may be refugees, business consultants, aid and development workers, immigrants or travellers. However, traditionally, second and foreign language learning, and its associated research, has been focused on children, teenagers and young adults. Mature adult language learners, especially those over 40 years of age, have featured only incidentally in much of our thinking about second language acquisition (SLA). Hence we have the question, 'Is there language acquisition after 40?', and this study, where older learners speak up.

This chapter is essentially a descriptive account, which aims to bring to light the reality of the experiences of five Asian learners of English in their middle years. We find that each of them articulates a clear theme, and that together they provide a perspective that illuminates a reality wider than the language learning process itself. Whether they achieve their proficiency goals, what their preferred learning styles are and how individual differences, including age, affect their learning are fascinating issues but are not the focus of this study. Rather, the focus is upon their beliefs, their experiences and the contexts of their learning.

## Background

Reviewing the literature on second language acquisition, we find that researchers have invested much in the investigation of the age factor in SLA, primarily to identify a critical, or at least a sensitive, period in the early years of life for the most effective outcomes. Singleton (1989), Ellis (1994), Singleton and Lengyel (1995) and Larsen-Freeman (2001) provide comprehensive summaries of the field as it stood in the 1990s and all agree that the evidence on age as a factor still appears confusing and inconclusive.

Larsen-Freeman (2001) draws attention to the fact that the bulk of SLA research over the years investigates the process from a biological or cognitive perspective rather than as it is socially constructed and experienced. She reiterates: 'As I wrote in 1991 we need more ethnographic research that takes the social context into account' (p. 24). Swain and Miccoli's (1994) study, investigating one 35-year-old Asian learner of English in an interactive small-group-learning context, is one of the few examples from the decade of such a study. A recent debate in *TESOL Quarterly* also underlines the lack of resolution on age and SLA (Marinova-Todd, Marshall and Snow 2000; Hyltenstam and Abrahamsson 2001). Marinova-Todd, Marshall and Snow's (2000) helpful overview of how past research findings have been at times misconstrued gives some clear pointers for the reading of studies in this area. They contend that the influence age seems to have on language learning is associated with age-related social, psychological, and educational factors, and 'not because of any critical period that limits the possibility of language learning by adults' (p. 28). A review of the literature in the nineties also reveals that studies focusing on the older language learner are isolated and of limited scope. Cook (1995, pp. 51–2) not only points out the methodological limitations of the research literature, but also reminds us that:

> age is a factor from birth to death. The relationship of age to second language acquisition is not just the difference between children and adults but might also involve second language acquisition in old age.

In particular, we do not yet know how learners fare at the mid to later end of the age continuum.

There are signs, however, of emerging research activity, albeit still within the psycholinguistic mainstream of SLA. Eckart (1995) reports on the motivation and background of adults with an average age of 45 studying a foreign language in a short intensive summer school. More recently Bongaerts *et al.* (1997) have investigated whether or not native-like speakers of a foreign language who had started learning post-puberty could be distinguished from native speakers. Phonology is also the focus of Pennington's (1998) examination of the nature of adult acquisition. Ehrman and Oxford (1995) isolated age as a factor in the context of their much wider study of SLA and individual differences with subjects between 25 and 52 years old. Their study suggested that 'it helps to have cognitive aptitude, effective learning habits, learning experience, motivation and self-confidence, as well as certain personality dispositions, but age alone is not an absolute barrier' (1995, p. 81).

To summarize then, a survey of the SLA research literature on the age factor reveals studies focused on, and rich in investigation of, individual cognitive and affective factors but with limited age range and with findings that are inconclusive. Overall, substantial studies of older language learners are notable for their absence, as are those that take social context into account.

## The study

For this preliminary look at the experience of language learners in their middle years, a study of several individual cases was chosen. Yin's (1994, p. 13) definition of a case study as 'an empirical enquiry that investigates a contemporary phenomenon within its real-life context, especially when the boundaries between phenomenon and context are not clearly evident' applies to this situation. We have the contemporary phenomenon of significant numbers of mature people learning another language either by choice or by force of circumstance and yet the interaction of the factors internal and external to the learner is far from clear (Bialystok 1994, p. 4). A case-study approach means the data cannot be generalized but can lead to a greater understanding of the dimensions of language learning in the real-life contexts of those of mature to older age. This approach is also congruent with Marinova-Todd, Marshall and Snow's proposal (2001) to move research from studying of groups of learners to working closely with individuals in order to be better informed about the impact of their situation of learning.

The five cases explored range in age from their late 30s to mid-50s (Figure 5.1). The five – four native speakers of Chinese and one of Korean – had been resident in New Zealand from one to four years. They were part of a significant flow of immigrants from East Asia into New Zealand in the nineties, drawn particularly by incentives offered by the New Zealand government to businesspeople, but also by perceptions of a healthy lifestyle and good education. They were all tertiary qualified and, without exception, currently experiencing language learning in a full-time, instructed setting and immersed in the target language, English. The names used here are not their real names.

The data are drawn from taped interviews comprising biographical information and responses to the set of open-ended guiding questions that follow:

- Could you explain your understanding of how adults learn a new language?
- What advantages do older adults have in learning a language?
- What disadvantages do they have?
- Tell me about yourself as a language learner.

| 'Name' | Age/ gender | first language | other languages | educational background | target language | purpose |
|--------|-------------|----------------|-----------------|------------------------|-----------------|---------|
| Jun Li | 39  F | Chinese | Russian | BEd. (Psych) | English | residence |
| Ling | 50s  M | Chinese | Russian | Dip (law) | English | residence/job |
| Zheng | 46  M | Chinese | — | BE | English | residence/job |
| Hong | 39  M | Chinese | Japanese/ German | BE | English | residence/job |
| Sunny | 40s  F | Korean | German | BA | English | residence/job |

**Figure 5.1** Participant profiles

- Are there any strategies/methods/techniques that you like to use if possible?
- Are there any you try to avoid?
- What advice would you give to a person over 40 starting to learn a new language?

The findings of the study are presented below in two forms. Firstly, there are profiles based on the tape transcript and the biographical details of each respondent. Secondly, interviewees' perspectives on how adults learn, the advantages and disadvantages for older learners, and their preferences in learning methods were collated and summarized along with their advice to others learning another language in later years.

## Profiles of the five learners

The direct quotations introducing each profile were selected both for their distinctiveness, and for their intensity. From the interviews, five key issues emerge: confidence, time, teacher input, learning style and self-esteem.

*Is there language acquisition after 40? Older learners speak up*

### Profile one: Jun Li and confidence

> If you think it's hard you will achieve only a low level . . . depends
> on confidence; everyone can be confident . . . If I spend some time
> for job I can't spend time for learning; it depends on what you
> want. This is for older people a problem.[1]

Jun Li, at almost 40, has been in New Zealand for a year. With a background of learning Russian at school and then graduating with a psychology major, she understands adult language learning to be similar
to child language learning, requiring concentration on oral skills, high-
frequency use and a substantial period of time.

Jun Li's experience of being an immigrant, a language learner, a mother
and homemaker, and without much money, challenged her to the core,
however. 'My husband was very angry: "This is an English country. If you
don't speak English, you can't do anything!"' After nine months of frustration and unhappiness ('I felt like a stupid, but I'm not a baby!'), she
realized her options were to stay in New Zealand with her husband and
son and persevere with English learning, or return to China without them.
She threw herself wholeheartedly into English learning, studying 19 hours
a week in class and over 10 independently. Two themes undeniably per-
meate her fragmented, but passionate communication: her recognition of
the time demand for language learning, and the importance of believing
in oneself ('If you too much say I can't do it, maybe you can't.').

### Profile two: Ling and time

> Learning a language costs much time – too much time, so I don't
> do any entertainment so dancing and travelling and meeting with
> friends I seldom do these things – cost a lot of time so I can sit in a
> room alone [and study]

Ling, in his 50s, has a part-time cleaning job, studies English around 40
hours a week (half of that instructed), and expects to be an effective real
estate agent in five years. His earnest commitment to language learning
is striking. For example, he recently took a native-speaker boarder into
his home to increase his (and his wife's) exposure to English. Ling sees
language learning as an all day, everyday, task. 'You must forget your
own language – pressure environment like in the army, then you can
learn in four years.'

Ling clearly states that one is never too old to learn English. 'If you
make a decision you can do it – you have to believe in yourself.' His
eagerness to learn may have its source in his earlier experience in China
of not getting a university education until his 40s, when he studied law.
'I like to learn anything especially English at present. That's why I over-

60

come this problem and I want to learn another – computer maybe . . . not enough time for everything. Later.'

Ling recognizes the advantages he has over his younger classmates: greater world knowledge, time free of childcare now and self-discipline. He addresses his disadvantages methodically: a part-time job to supplement the family income, use of vocabulary cards and notebook to activate his memory, instructed learning to provide his preferred learning environment. '[With] strict teachers, students have a pressure to learn, more structure and push you to learn English.' Ling's ownership of the whole enterprise – the time, the financial cost, the choices made, his belief in himself – undoubtedly feeds into his present huge energy for learning English.

### Profile three: Zheng and teacher input

> You need a teacher to organize everything – you can't do it by yourself. You have no experience how to learn that language. You also need pressure. Adults don't need more pressure than others but need some.

As he speaks Zheng sprinkles his comments with examples of how his teachers have helped him: A helped with writing; L banned bilingual dictionaries; M insisted on listening directly to authentic material; B modelled grouping of new vocabulary from a written text. An engineer from China, Zheng has been in New Zealand three years – the first in a mainstream undergraduate programme, the second and third in full-time English classes, and hopefully returning to mainstream study next year.

Reflecting on his learning, he identifies a poor memory and slow reaction as the hurdles he faces ('my own language is stronger, I need to think before I can say'). But he is excited about the changes he has made in learning strategies. Before, he relied on his Chinese–English dictionary, writing a paragraph took hours, he avoided the telephone, and watching television was boring. Now he uses an English–English dictionary ('I was angry, but later found it very good'), writes with a structure in mind and a time limit, speaks in English for up to an hour on the phone with classmates, and includes television news in his regular review cycle of finding the same information in newspaper, television and radio.

Zheng has learnt the rewards of persistence, seeing this as an advantage older learners have. He warns against long breaks in learning ('If you stop for a year or even a month you forget things'), citing his own experience of three weeks' illness. Currently Zheng spends about 40 hours a week in class and related independent study, as well as using English in his environment – the phone calls, the news media. He closes with 'When I was young I never needed to do homework. I remembered everything from the teacher.' And he has now added effective strategies to his language learning formula.

### Profile four: Hong and learning style

> I'm used to learning in a formal way. Now I need to learn from listening . . . Sometimes I think if we were learning another subject with [NZ] students it would be better for talking with them.

After 18 months in New Zealand, Hong, an engineer from China, expects it will be two to three more years before he can enter the workforce at a satisfactory level. Currently spending around 35 hours a week in class and related independent study, he develops his listening skill for a couple more hours a day, using the local media. Speaking opportunities are harder to find, but Hong has been innovative in visits to the Citizens Advice Bureau, real estate 'open homes' promotions, selling in a local flea market and using the telephone. 'I try to contact local people as much as possible. If you have many chances to talk with local people every day then one year would be enough [to learn English], but it is impossible [to get such sufficient exposure]. Even if you live with New Zealanders, it is still impossible to talk with them all day.' This awareness comes from comparing his situation with that of his son: 'My son has better conditions to learn – he has local people to speak with.'

However, Hong readily identifies advantages he has as an older learner. Learning culture and customs is easier, as is reading because of a wider world knowledge. Adults also know time is important and that every opportunity must be taken. For Hong a poor memory, first language dominance and difficulties with pronunciation continue to plague him, but small successes along the way give him confidence. 'If every time you have a test you pass then you will be more confident . . . volunteer job in the flea market was very helpful for me to understand local people and becoming confident.'

### Profile five: Sunny and self-esteem

> When I came to New Zealand, people thought I had no education. I'm worried about that. In Korea, I was on the board of trustees [of daughter's school], but here I was just a helper because my English not good enough. . . I like helping, a *real* helper.

Sunny, in her 40s and a Mathematics graduate, has been in New Zealand three and a half years, and only now is studying full time. Her focus has been settling her family, learning English by reading and talking with neighbours and her daughter's school contacts, but now she feels the need for greater stimulation and challenge. Sunny finds everything in class is very useful, and in spite of frequently being exhausted after four to five hours a day in class, she has never been bored. As a disciplined and organized learner, she expects to be able to make progress on her own after a year of formal instruction. A long-term commitment to learning English is part of Sunny's strategy: 'If you don't continue for over three years full time at least, it's not worth starting,' she advises. This time frame seems to arise from her perception that language learning is the same for older and younger people except that older people take more time. 'Apart from that, it is individual differences, not age' that make any difference.

For Sunny, then, belief in her own abilities, a generous time frame, recognition of the demands of her family and making the most of the best learning opportunities she can find combine to make her a realistic and focused learner. 'If I find something interesting then I can do it.'

## An overview of findings from the interviews

This section summarizes the participants' comments on the interview questions and then attempts an overview of their perceptions of learning another language at this stage in life.

### *Beliefs about how adults learn another language*

Responses to this topic embraced a range of views. Hong believed that adults have to learn in a different way from children, and that it is more difficult because of memory and pronunciation problems. Zheng felt strongly the need for a teacher to guide adults and to provide 'pressure'. Several said adults had to try harder than younger learners do, and that adults need a long time and a lot of time. However, this length and quantity of time was also seen as a feature of the way children learn another language and the learners considered being immersed in the target language as highly desirable for adults too. Thus, there was support for the view that adults learn in the same way as children. Sunny was keen to make this point at the close of the interview: 'Younger and older people is the same, but older study [take] more time. Apart from that it is individual differences, not age.' Ling also was quite clear: '[One] is never too old to learn English – so for all old people it is useful.'

### *Advantages perceived for older language learners*

Four advantages were articulated: general world knowledge, previous language knowledge, self-discipline and time. Of these, four of the learners mentioned the life experience and world knowledge of mature adults, and only one identified prior grammatical knowledge. Those with no dependent children found they had time to put into language learning, and several saw their ability to be disciplined as an advantage that adults have.

### Disadvantages perceived for older language learners

Time again emerges, but as a negative factor now. Adults frequently have other demands on their time – a need to earn a living, to maintain a family with its various needs and the time taken up by a job. 'It's not easy because we have other things to do, not only language – housework, a job' (Ling) and 'when people come to a new country they have living problems, not much money, this is not like children. A teenager has nothing [else] to do' (Jun Li). A cluster of potentially age-related phenomena was also problematic. All five learners stated that their memory was poor. Some mentioned slow reactions, poor pronunciation and the influence of their first language. Overall there was a consensus about the perceived disadvantages, with lack of time and memory failure being dominant.

### Themselves as language learners

Interviewees took this prompt as an opportunity to talk about their learning environments. Several explained that they had chosen to be in a class at this point, because they felt the need of guidance, of pressure and a structure to their learning. Zheng particularly articulated the guidance given by several of his teachers as to useful strategies: brainstorming before writing, use of a monolingual dictionary, following lexical strings as an aid to reading. All three post-intermediate learners volunteered that their learning style had changed since coming to classes in New Zealand. Their experience before had been formal and based on written texts. 'I'm used to learning in a formal way . . . I could spell and understand, but I couldn't understand it spoken. So now I think I need to learn from listening' (Hong).

### Preferred strategies, methods or techniques

Predictably, quite a range of practices came through here, centring on oral language and vocabulary development. The two with a slightly lower proficiency level particularly mentioned substantial use of a dictionary, use of a vocabulary notebook or cards and repetitive review. The three post-intermediate learners focused on their oral and aural skills: listening to songs, talking on the phone, watching television news three times in one evening to recycle the topics, finding opportunities to speak with local people at the Citizens Advice Bureau, selling in a local street market, 'open homes' for real estate sales and helping in a daughter's school. Ling explained a remarkable and far-reaching strategy: 'We just moved house a week ago, because [Chinese] flatmates not easy [to learn English]. Now Kiwi guy, 21 year old, very kind, lives with us; my wife is very happy to mix with a New Zealander so she can learn English.'

Language games in class, decontextualized vocabulary lists and conversation classes were things Hong and Zheng avoided. Zheng confessed to having to force himself to talk to native speakers. The other three learners said they consciously tried to use every method they could.

### Advice to learners over 40

Two of the key pieces of advice they gave were the need for confidence, and the need to commit large amounts of time, both on a daily basis and long term. They made comments such as: 'confidence – if you too much say I can't do it maybe you can't do it – no soul, no power' (Jun Li), and from Hong: '[working in a volunteer job] was very helpful for me to understand local people – becoming confident' and 'if every time you had a test you pass then you will be more confident. If you fail then you feel less confident.' Ling advised: 'If you make a decision you can do it – you have to believe in yourself.'

The need for commitment of time was expressed as: 'If you don't continue for over three years full time at least it is not worth starting,' (Sunny) and 'If one could learn English you must do always work hard all day continual, not stop. If stop maybe forget,' and 'Some advertisement say: in 100 days you can command English language. Not true not true' (Ling).

Other suggestions targeted the process of learning: review regularly, find a good teacher, obtain a good dictionary, try to learn in the target language context and get a job if possible, even as a volunteer. Jun Li provided a telling insight: 'If you want go high level, you maybe get middle level; if you go middle level, you get low level.' In other words, realistically one achieves less than one would like so if you set only a low goal, then you will achieve even less than that. It is best to aim high and then you will achieve something quite good.

## Discussion

At this point, we stand back and look at the big picture. We have described and examined in some detail the perceptions of five adults who have committed to learning another language in the midst of a stage of life usually marked by stability, productivity and achievement. Is there anything remarkable in what they have said? Does it match the insights and findings of second language acquisition research? What questions filter through? We are not looking for conclusions here. Our intent is to discern issues worth further exploration and to identify, in the limited but rich data available, the potential for significant insights.

The informants' beliefs about how adults learn a new language, and the advantages and disadvantages they identified are clouded by the use of the imprecise terms 'older' and 'younger'. We cannot always be sure what was intended – whether comments referred to adults and children or to middle-aged and young adults. In spite of this, we discern a more positive view of adult language learning than is generally expressed in popular thought. The only concessions made cluster around the time needed, both in intensity and in length, and the effects of physiological ageing on memory, auditory competence and speed of response. This latter cluster coincides completely with the 'at a disadvantage in only a few respects' that Singleton (1989, p. 263) concludes concerning the 'young-old'. But the possibilities that older learners may need more time, or learn at a slower rate, are not a particular feature in the litera-ture. In fact, Ellis (1994, p. 491) found evidence that adults may have an initial advantage over children where rate is concerned, especially in grammar. This is another example of where the meaning of 'old' or 'adult' and 'young' needs more precise definition before we can make any progress.

However, the 'time needed' issue stands out as a significant dimension of these learners' experiences, and this is not at all predicted in the research literature. Time surfaces consistently as they talk: in their advice to others embarking on language learning in their middle years, in refer-ences to the daily practice required, in the opportunity cost of not only taking full-time lessons, but also, the consolidation out of class, and in their recognition of the years it takes to reach even modest proficiency goals. Three explanations of this perception come to mind. It may be, for instance, that the time required is simply a shock in contrast to their pre-vious learning experiences in other disciplines. Or, is it that people learn-ing another language at this stage of life do actually take longer than younger learners, all other things being equal? But then again, it is pos-sible that the time commitment common to any language learning assumes much bigger proportions in middle age because of social pres-sures to be productive, because of life in general becoming more com-plicated, and the years becoming more precious as time runs out. This is an important issue to explore. The potential for learners to understand the time dimension better will bring with it major dividends in setting appropriate language goals and time frames, together with recognition of, and planning for, the realities inherent in the task, the context and themselves.

Another issue implicit in the data and worthy of more exploration is the level and intensity of their decision-making. Not only is their initial decision to learn the language a big one, but their ongoing decisions about how they will learn and about the balance between language learning and the rest of their lives are constant and potentially stressful. There is no one else taking the responsibility for them, no employer requiring it, no parent encouraging it, no government paying for it: the decision is theirs alone. Also unexplored in this study is these immigrants' awareness of what their initial decision to emigrate was in fact committing them to. Did they realize the scope of what they were embarking on?

The theme of confidence and self-esteem is another dimension addressed with some intensity in the interviews, possibly signalling that, for learners in their middle years plus, we have a particular issue. There is potential here for more insights from the more general field of adult learning to be usefully applied to the SLA experience. The SLA literature shows some work has been done. Wajnryb (1988) and Swain and Miccoli (1994) have alerted us to the possibly direct link in the language learning process between vulnerable self-esteem and the middle and older adult years. Lightbown and Spada (1993, p. 39) helpfully point out that such variables as self-esteem present a confused picture in SLA research, and this could be explained in part by the intrinsic multidimensional nature of language learning. Personality variables seem to be consistently related to 'the acquisition of communicative competence' and not grammatical accuracy or language knowledge.

However, the experience of these learners requires this theme to be taken seriously even if the extent to which lack of confidence and self-esteem are age-related is not known. To some degree, sooner or later, it is likely any language learner will need to deal with this personal challenge. Norton's (2001) report on the relationship of participation levels to identity and communities of belonging for five language learners is relevant here. Although not explicitly in an SLA and age frame, a finding such as the following is undoubtedly part of the older adult experience: 'while language learners may be comfortable being positioned as newcomers to the knowledge and skills of the grammar teacher, some may resist being positioned as newcomers to the practices of being an adult, such as renting an apartment, going to the doctor and taking a bus' (2001, p. 170). Perhaps the unique issue for the mature learner is that, as with the time demand discussed above, a challenge to one's self-esteem, identity and confidence is unexpected.

A final dimension emerging from these learner profiles is, not surprisingly, the learning process itself. The nature of teacher input, of the learning environment, of the resources, the learners' preferred strategies and approaches are all identified as significant influences in their learning. This matches the findings of Swain and Miccoli (1994), who suggest that the social component of language learning is as significant as the cognitive. Their adult learner struggled with the interactive, collaboratively structured classroom experience she was exposed to and came close to dropping out, perceiving herself to be a poor language learner. With support and conscious reflection on the processes, she was able to distinguish the social from the cognitive dimensions and act to turn things around. The five learners in this study also described how their learning environment impacted on their achievement, indicating a degree of awareness of factors conducive to their language learning.

## Conclusion

Yes, there is language acquisition after 40. The reality is that people well past their youth need to, want to and do learn new languages. In this chapter we have captured something of their experience. What they chose to speak up about has revealed not so much new angles but new emphases, ones that do not particularly feature in the literature. By listening carefully to their beliefs and experiences we have found that the significance both of time needed and of challenges to confidence and self-esteem was largely unpredicted and profound. Use of a methodology where the learner is provided a framework in which to reflect aloud on their realities has revealed new emphases. This underlines the value of autobiographical material in the study of SLA and mature age learners.

Although popular wisdom has been pessimistic about the ability of mature age learners to achieve even modest goals, there are signs here that Marinova-Todd, Marshall and Snow (2000, pp. 27–8) are correct in pressing for a re-formulation of studies in age and second language learning. With some careful attention to both research and informed support, the total learning experience and, as a result, the outcomes could be significantly improved for the over-40s language learner.

## Note

1. The data extracts in this chapter are taken from verbatim transcriptions of interviews conducted in English. These extracts have not been edited for grammatical accuracy.

# 6  An Arabic-speaking English learner's path to autonomy through reading

*Diane Malcolm*

The recent focus on the development of learner autonomy as a feature of lifelong language learning has highlighted the strong influence of a learner's beliefs, which may be, in turn, a product of previous training, cultural practices and the learner's own experiences (Horwitz 1987). Much of the research on language learning beliefs and their effects on the learner's use of strategies has taken the form of interviews and question-naires conducted with foreign students enrolled in English language programmes, especially at the tertiary level and in English-speaking countries (e.g., Wenden 1986a, 1986b, 1987; Oxford 1990). The stated aim of much of this research has been to enable teachers and learners to use the insights gained from an examination of their beliefs to develop an effective set of strategies to improve their language learning. Many of these studies have also focused on the strategies of successful learners (e.g., Rubin 1975; Naiman *et al.* 1978) with a similar purpose of equip-ping less successful learners, through example and training, with better means to learn a language.

Perhaps because much of the interest in this area has been concerned with heightening awareness of learner strategies for pedagogical pur-poses, there have been fewer studies relating to how learners' beliefs, and the strategies derived from them, develop in relation to the changing con-texts of their life and language learning experiences over time. In short, although it has been stressed that 'learner beliefs are inherently unstable' (Benson and Lor 1998), how they evolve into personal theories of effec-tive language learning is not well documented. The present study details the progress of one learner, over several years and through a variety of changing contexts, in developing an effective set of strategies for learn-ing English and describes how his current strongly held belief in the value of reading as the 'key' to language development came about. While it must be stressed that the story of his path to autonomy in learning English is unique, it lends support to the notion that the set of beliefs an individual language learner holds is not static but is modified and refined in relation to changing contexts and experiences. The beliefs and prac-tices articulated by this learner are also discussed in relation to those reported in Benson and Lor (1998) and Wenden (1987), bearing in mind the fact that those studies relate to beliefs derived from groups of learn-ers, and not from one individual, as is the case here.

## Background and study design

The study was the result of a collaboration between myself and a 24-year-old male Saudi Arabian fifth-year medical student, Hamad, at the Arabian Gulf University in Bahrain. Unusually among my former students, Hamad has made a point of seeking me out for guidance in language learning matters over the past several years. His readiness to analyse and pursue his English learning goals singled him out as an appropriate candidate for this study, which he undertook willingly. Four half-hour to one-hour interview sessions, which were tape-recorded and transcribed, were conducted in English over a two-week period. Prior to the first interview, Hamad was given a set of questions to consider (see Appendix 1). He was also asked to complete the Strategy Inventory for Language Learning (Oxford 1990). His results indicated high overall strategy use, with little variation among strategy groups (Appendix 2).

## Hamad's story

Hamad began learning English as a school subject in Saudi Arabia then continued his formal study of English at two university preparatory programmes: one intensive semester at King Fahad University of Petroleum and Minerals (KFUPM) in Dhahran, Saudi Arabia, prior to being admitted to the medical college, and then for two terms as part of his pre-medical year courses (Year 1) at Arabian Gulf University (AGU) in Bahrain. He thus completed his formal language training as part of his academic requirements in 1997. In addition, Hamad attended a two-week intensive English course in the USA in 1994, where he lived with a family and spent an additional week in a hotel. He also recently completed a course at a private language institute in Bahrain. Many friends and colleagues at AGU who are fluent bilingual Arabic–English speakers have also had a strong influence in his English practice, beliefs and assumptions. Hamad has also been exposed to English through his medical studies, although he strongly discounts its influence on his language development.

### Initial beliefs

One theme that takes a central place in Hamad's beliefs about language learning is his conviction that reading is the key to his English language development.

> When I want to talk about learning English, how to learn English.
> When I joined the university I discovered in a moment that reading

is the most important and without it you can't learn any other skill.[1]

This discovery appears almost self-evident, in an academic context. However, as the discussion proceeded, it became evident that there were many layers of complexity to this simple concept. Hamad points to the role of reading as a means to acquire information:

> It's not just about learning English. It's how to . . . how you can get the idea from the whole subject. How to make summary about all what you read.

He also describes the long, tortuous pathway he followed to reach his present conviction that 'reading is the basic of the English'. The roots of his struggle with reading began in intermediate school, when he began learning English as a school subject. Reading passages were part of the syllabus:

> We just had a questions about a paragraph in front of us. We read a paragraph and answer . . . they were very direct forward questions. We just copy it down. Even when you don't understand any single word in that sentence. You just correlate the words.

At this stage of his language learning, Hamad admits that he didn't understand many things but he was, nonetheless, very skilled at getting high marks. There were some changes in the methods of teaching reading in high school: 'Now we have reading but they don't ask us something we can just copy it. So now you have to understand . . . You have to read more . . . to understand. It was interesting. I liked it so much.' However, he is in general very dismissive of the benefits of his school learning of English: 'What I've learned in school was nothing.' He reserves particular condemnation for the reading part of the syllabus: 'This is one of the biggest mistake I ever seen in the reading part. They don't take care of reading.'

Hamad's attitude to reading began to change in his college years. In his intensive course at KFUPM, he spent one hour a day on reading. Nonetheless, the attitude to reading engendered by his school experience remained:

> I have a whole book. Reading book . . . But, at the beginning, the reading book I don't use it. Why? What they gonna ask? Just reading and answer the questions. That's it.

He had a rude awakening after the first test, when he discovered he couldn't answer the questions: 'It's very hard. Even though if I read it twice . . . and I don't have time. Especially their exams . . . if you have 100 questions you have 20 minutes.'

Reading took second place at that time to being a fluent speaker of English, which Hamad equated with being good at English. Thus, Hamad was not much affected by what his reading teacher at KFUPM was trying to teach him:

> You have to learn how to read fast and I discovered that the teacher taught us how to do it, but I didn't give them my complete attention.

Rather, his observation of fast speakers of English, whom he assumed were 'good at English', a notion he later revised, cemented the belief that acquiring vocabulary through reading was the way to become as fluent as those he admired.

> The idea in my mind was you have to learn more vocab. You'll be a good English speaker . . . 'Cause when you're gonna learn vocab, you will understand more. You can understand how they talk.

As a result, he began to tackle reading as a means to acquire vocabulary for oral fluency:

> The most important thing for me which I was always dream of was . . . to talk in English. This is what was affecting my reading. Because when I read, now I wanna be a good speaker. I wanna talk English fluently. I translate every single word I see in the page which took a lot of effort and took a long time, which made me so bored from reading. I don't like to read. It takes a lot of effort.

Because of the effort and time involved, and because this process was not producing the hoped-for results, Hamad became demoralized:

> The most important point here, that you feel down. And you doubting your way. I still read but I don't get benefit. We always want to see the results very fast . . . when I start doubting that way or any way I use I just quit.

### The need to study in English

The idea that reading was important had taken root during his study at KFUPM, but it wasn't until Hamad came to AGU that he was able to formulate and carry out an effective strategy for using reading to gain English proficiency. Here he questioned his previous beliefs that reading is a useless skill and that reading is a means of acquiring the vocabulary needed to be a fluent speaker when he encountered Arabic-speaking English learners who were fluent yet had graduated from government schools, just like him: 'I came here, I see different students with me the same batch, talking fluently, very good. And they learned English in a normal school as I do.' So he asked them how they had achieved this:

> One of them . . . told me: 'I read a lot English . . . I read stories.'
> I'm like: 'All of this vocab, you learned from reading stories?' He's
> like: 'Yes, not all of it, but most of it, from reading stories.'

Nonetheless, Hamad is sceptical. 'When you go to any person in the
world he will tell you the same ways . . . read, watch movies . . . okay,
they are right, but I don't feel it's a good way because it will, in a way,
restricted me.'

In addition to encountering fluent non-native speakers, Hamad came
to realize at AGU the demands that studying in English would put on his
abilities, and how little his previous training had prepared him for this:

> I tried to accommodate to this atmosphere, 'I have to study in
> English', and this affected my studying so much, because I can't
> understand. There's a big difference between studying biology in
> English and in Arabic, even [if] they have the same information.
> The way I studied biology in Arabic . . . it's just memorize
> information and I have to copy them in my paper. But in English
> here I notice. I can't study . . . in this way. Because I have two
> things to do. I have to understand the sentence, then I memorize it.
> Which consumed a lot of time. It was very hard. I blamed my
> English . . . even with my lowest mark.

The urgent need to develop effective reading strategies for study purposes and the long-established desire to become a fluent speaker of
English (which meant being good at English) pushed Hamad to search
for ways to achieve these ends:

> 'I have to do something about my English because this is my
> future.' I believed that practice was very important. But I need to
> do something with my practice. What to do? I started to find ways.
> 'Let me try to read a story.' I felt very happy at the beginning, then
> I started to feel bored suddenly. I don't exaggerate . . . just two
> pages I spent 35, 40 minutes.

Still influenced by his belief that being good at English meant knowing
a lot of vocabulary, Hamad conscientiously looked up every new word
he came across. The amount of time consumed in this task reached epic
proportions, and yet no progress was being made in either understanding biology or becoming fluent in English. He began to doubt his ability
to continue with his medical studies:

> With the biology in Year One here, I started at the beginning to
> translate every single word. The whole afternoon I'm still on the
> first page. 'I'm not good enough for medicine,' which affected me.
> 'I'm not good in English. I'm not good . . . to do medicine. Just
> one page.' And I can see the pages of Year Two, Unit One. They
> have 100, 170 a week. How can I finish all that?

At this point, Hamad realized the limitations of his initial method of translating every new word. He relied upon the advice of his more fluent friends not to translate, but rather to just read.

> I started . . . I don't translate any word, just I try to read. Ok? Because this is the way. Translating is wrong. I've heard this from all my friends who were very good in English: 'Don't translate in Arabic. This is very wrong. Try to do it alone.'

Heeding their advice, Hamad ploughed through his readings: 'I started to read, to read, to read and I used this way.' However, the results were disastrous: 'I failed the first unit because of this.' Now instead of hunting for every unknown word, Hamad's strategy was to read on regardless of understanding:

> For example, the paragraph [has] six sentences. I understood the first one. I didn't get the second. I didn't get the third. I understood the fourth, I didn't understand the fifth. I go on. At the end, you ask me about the page, I don't understand anything. But my way, in translating every single word, doesn't work. And this one, all of them they use it. And it works and I failed because I didn't understand anything. But I was reading, reading, reading.

This he attributes to his failure to understand correctly the advice he had been given:

> I took it wrong. I understood it wrongly. I used to read and I skip. I missed the meaning of the sentence, which was really wrong.

Reading fast without getting the meaning of what he is reading was ineffective, so Hamad revised his strategy to include selective dictionary use.

> If I have to open the dictionary for this word, single word, to understand the whole idea, so I have to open the dictionary here. Even though I will waste time but I have to do it because I will miss the whole information.

This marked the beginning of an effective reading strategy which he arrived at through much painful trial and error. He also attributed the breakthrough to the realization that understanding, not translating, is the key to effective reading.

> I missed the way of reading until I . . . started to read stories. Now when I read a story, from inside of me, I want to understand what's going on. So if I don't understand the sentence, I go back. I'm like: 'What does that mean?'

Although translation still is a part of this technique, the dictionary is now used to check understanding, not to generate long lists of quickly forgotten vocabulary.

> Still here I translate new words in the sentence. Not like before at the
> beginning – translate every single word. I felt bored at the beginning
> but I felt . . . that it affects my normal studying. Now when I study if
> I don't understand the sentence I go back again. It's like a usual now
> in my personality. So it affected my studying, also positively.

Another refinement of this strategy took place when Hamad realized, on
my advice, that it wasn't essential for him to use a dictionary for every
single sentence that contained an unknown word. 'I noticed I get bored
from the story because I still take time. Then after I talked to you I
noticed that I don't have to translate that single word if I understand the
sentence, which I found it very, very helpful.'

### Reading as the key to learning English

With these effective strategies mastered, finally Hamad was able to use
reading as a key to develop his English and to study more effectively as
well. He summarized his rules for reading:

> If you do understand the sentence, go on. But if you don't
> understand, don't move. Just open the dictionary even although
> you will use the dictionary for every single word in the sentence.
> You have to open the dictionary if you don't understand. This is
> what I found very helpful. And I finished books. Not one, not 2, 3,
> 4, 5, 6. I'm not bored. Because I'm reading.

The success he has experienced in applying these strategies has paid off
in increasing his confidence in reading:

> If I found myself confused I go and I open the dictionary. And now
> I finished 3, 4 pages and once I use the dictionary, which is
> different and that gives you more confidence so you read more.

Having mastered reading, Hamad now is able to use it as a spring-
board to improve his other English skills:

> When I read I try to not read silently. Why? Because to learn how
> to pronounce the words. It helps me to focus. It helps me to not
> my thinking go here and here, ok? Which one of my aims. To
> pronounce to say the words in proper way which it gives you
> confident in front of people.

Vocabulary acquisition is also improved through his reading, along with
other language skills:

> I feel very, very happy when I heard a word I just read it and read
> it in the book, which make me read more.

> You can see the different meaning of words in the reading.
> Writing. You can't write without read. Even the grammar.

Over the years, Hamad's beliefs have evolved:

> I discovered different subjects in reading. Different aims also, it plays an important role. Different ways in learning English. All of this in one ball. How to read, my aim in learning English. Don't be fast. All of this I took it in two years to know it or I got to be convinced in two years. I started exactly in KFUPM because my idea about reading at that time it was zero. I'm like: 'This is a useless skill.' And after no. It started like that. Reading helps you in all subjects.

### The habit of reading

Hamad's conviction that reading is key is tempered by cautions about the difficulty of becoming a reader, and his struggle to break his own habits:

> It's so hard to make yourself a good reader. It's an issue alone. Separate issue. How to read. Reading it wasn't one of my favourite hobbies . . . In my free time I do this and this, but I don't read. I have to convince myself to take it step by step until I can make it as one of my habits. To read.

He speculates that the cultural patterns of reading in Arabic, especially in his country, have had an influence on his reluctance to read:

> This is a big difference . . . I will not say in general, but it's true. When I go to the United State or UK I can see the small children when they are in the queue, they have books to read. This is in their life. Here, we don't have this. This is why, now, in this age, you will tell me, 'Go and read . . . a story.' [How can I] if I'm not a reader?

His experience as a reader has also led him to modify his original belief that knowing English means being a fast and fluent speaker of the language:

> Maybe you'll never be fluent as much as them because it's different. Someone who was using English since he was . . . four years, it's different from me. I just learned English in 3 or 4 years. But still, you can be better than them even in many fields. English is not just talking, not just speaking. A lot of fields in English.

Furthermore, his experience as a medical student showed him that even fluent speakers of English were not guaranteed success in their studies:

> Later on, I notice it's not just English. I didn't get this bad mark because I didn't understand just English. A lot of students, I discovered later, which talk fluently, English I meant, they didn't

get good marks. And here the idea that there is a difference
between talk and use English . . . raised in my mind. I look at
learning English in wrong way. If you want to learn English, this is
not the way. It's not with the same way I'm doing now. Just I
wanna talk, learning vocab. No.

Hamad described what he considered suitable reading material:

> It's a very simple story which helps me a lot to learn English and I
> enjoy them . . . maybe for a normal person, American . . . they are
> boring. But what make them, very good for me because I can feel
> or I can see my improvement. I found them very helpful. If some of
> my friend see the book they're like: 'Oh, this is for children.' I'm
> like: 'This is for me, because they have simple English which I use
> the words outside . . . so I can see the benefit.' Specifically I feel
> very happy when I heard a word I read it in the book, which
> makes me read more.

Hamad has developed confidence in his ability to apply his reading
strategies to other text types, although he does not choose to do so. For
example, he has tried and given up reading the newspaper:

> I tried. I open the newspaper. I couldn't. This is what made me be
> so sure about that you have to enjoy it. Like one column here it's
> talking about anything . . . interested . . . like 'lion went out of the
> cage'. Just you understand the first, you want to understand the
> rest. I wanna know because it's interested story and it's real. But at
> the end, I looked at the newspaper, I didn't read much of it. It's
> useless. I don't see that I just read that part. Because it's not
> satisfying.

Nonetheless, he is sure he would be able to read the newspaper efficiently
if he had the time and inclination as he now knows how to read it:

> I know if I tried more, I would be reading now more. That's
> because it's a repeated vocabulary. But I didn't do that because . . .
> I'm trying to find a solution that makes me happy. It's not my
> major job in this day to read the newspaper.

The same belief in repeated vocabulary was a factor in equipping him to
deal with the vast amount of reading in medicine. When I asked him how
he overcame the problem of 100 to 170 pages of reading material a week
in the medical phase he replied:

> I know how it went, but it's not easy to tell a person even now. For
> example, I told many Year 2 students . . . 'You'll spend a lot of
> time to read one page, but later on you will see yourself reading
> more. You know why? Because you will get to know the way you
> read anatomy. You will be exposed to the same vocabulary, so you
> will understand what's going on. And now if you read one page in

> two hours, later on you will read one page in one minute, or two
> minutes, not more than that because you already exposed to this
> vocabulary.'

Hamad now has complete confidence in his ability to handle any and all types of reading and complete faith in his method of improving his English through reading stories and applying the strategies he learned to all other reading tasks.

## Discussion

The description of the evolving personal theory of reading as the key to the development of Hamad's autonomy in learning English has been given at length, reflecting the importance he himself attributed to it. It is evident that the position that reading occupies in his personal theory of language learning underwent many modifications, from a 'useless' activity to the central role it now plays. It is also the case that, as this is a retrospective biography, Hamad's current belief in the importance of reading has probably had an effect on his recollection of earlier-held beliefs. While he began his history chronologically, from his earliest experiences at school, frequently throughout our interviews he interspersed comments relating to his current state of knowledge about the importance of reading. He was very aware that it was a long-drawn-out process, and his struggle led him to suggest other students facing the same predicament should be shown the easiest way in reading. If they become convinced, as he was at the beginning, that reading is hard, they will give it up. It is also worth noting that Hamad's attitudes to learning English, reflected in his selection of strategies, can be related to his increasing personal maturity. The change in attitude from the impatient, easily bored secondary school student, to the mature and analytical young adult, who has experienced some setbacks, affects his choice of methods, as does the lessening need for approbation from his peers. For example, in his early choices he is much swayed by his admiration for 'fast talkers', but later is content to choose reading material that suits his goals, although his friends may consider it childish.

During the evolution of his personal theory, Hamad formulated, tested and revised many beliefs, both similar and different to those in other studies, specifically the 'explicit prescriptive beliefs' described in Wenden (1987), i.e., use the language, learn about the language and personal factors, and the three groups of beliefs about principles and methods of language learning described in Benson and Lor (1998), i.e., those related to work, method and motivation.

The first learner belief that was found to be prevalent in Benson and

Lor, although not in Wenden, was the importance of work, or putting in effort as essential to success. Although he does not allude directly to the need for applying effort in order to progress in learning English, it is clear that Hamad has expended a great deal of effort to arrive at his current level. However, he also acknowledges the pointlessness of applying effort without results, as when he gave up on looking up every word in the dictionary. His main concern was with finding a method of practice that was productive and enjoyable, because he recognized that otherwise he would quickly lose motivation and begin to doubt his way was right.

One term that surfaced frequently in Hamad's discussion of developing skills such as listening and speaking as well as reading was *enjoyment*. Activities that he didn't enjoy were quickly shelved, as were those that took up too much of his time. Those opportunities to practise he found most productive were the ones in which he had a personal stake or could see the relevance to his own life. For example, he enjoyed the speaking classes he took as part of his course at a local institute because the discussion was related to 'real life', not just classroom drills.

Many of Hamad's beliefs can be related to method, the second category discussed in Benson and Lor. As they describe it, method relates to the 'conditions under which work will be successful' (Benson and Lor 1998, p. 26), including having a teacher, building a good foundation, exposing yourself to the language, etc. As his history makes clear, there were several key stages where Hamad sought and used advice from a teacher or other language informant, such as a fluent non-native speaker friend. He did not consider regular classroom practice to be very valuable in developing his own methods, even for the period when he was enrolled in English classes. In fact, he remarked that he had been taught skills that he didn't apply and understood only after several years of personal effort. However, he did feel the need for more explanation as well as more practice, as is evidenced by his choosing to take a course at a language institute recently.

Although in Wenden's study the need to think in English was a frequently reported belief, Hamad was unable to fathom exactly what that meant. He cites it as one of the pieces of advice provided by his language learning sources along with 'read the newspaper, watch TV, listen to the news, watch movies' and other regularly reported strategies, which he felt had little or no application to the theory he arrived at. Dutifully, he attempted to follow the advice but often found it contributed insignificantly to his progress, and was often counterproductive. In fact, he is critical of the value of such advice in that it may be misleading to beginning learners, who may quickly become bored, as Hamad did. They will feel they have wasted their time with little benefit, and this may lead to a drop in motivation, self-doubt and ultimately to rejection of this method of practice.

Hamad also does not now appear to subscribe to the belief expressed by some learners in the other studies that a good foundation or knowing a lot about different aspects of language are important for his language development. For example, some learners in Wenden's study stated: 'Grammar is important to learn' and 'English consists of words and I think I should learn more vocabulary' (Wenden 1987, p. 106). In that study, 'learn grammar/vocabulary' was the second most frequent 'explicit prescriptive belief'. The following statements are typical of the learners in the Benson and Lor study: 'When we decide to learn, we should devote time to construct our foundations, like having clear concepts of grammar, word patterns, etc.'; 'When learning a language, I think I should consider several aspects. They are reading, writing, listening and speaking. I cannot ignore one of them. Otherwise, there is an absence of one face for a box.' As we have seen, Hamad considers reading to be the one skill that contributes to the development of all aspects of language learning, at least as he uses it. Nonetheless, like the learners in the other studies, Hamad does believe that understanding your aims or goals is one of the bases in developing an effective set of language learning strategies.

The final set of beliefs, reported in Benson and Lor under the heading of motivation, and characterized by Wenden as personal factors, is one Hamad alludes to often. He relates how he 'feels down' when he compares himself to more fluent speakers and how he doubted his way when he met with failure. His frequent use of affective terms such as 'happy' and 'confident' express his sensitivity to the emotional needs of a language learner. He is very self-critical, for example, when comparing himself to more fluent speakers in his college setting. Overall, Hamad recounts being cast down by his failures and buoyed up by his successes. In fact, he attributes much of his progress to the assurance he got from others that he was on the right track.

## Conclusion

Because this study relates to the experiences of just one learner it cannot be assumed that groups of learners or even another individual of the same language and educational background would behave in the same way. What studies such as this one can demonstrate is that a learner's beliefs, like so many other aspects of language learning, are in a state of flux, constantly being revised and modified through the interplay of a wide variety of influences. A 'snapshot' of Hamad's beliefs in Year 1 at AGU, for example, would have yielded a very different image to the current one. Furthermore, this learner biography supports Benson's conclusion that self-management of learning plays an important role in a language learner's developing proficiency (Benson 2001, p. 65).

Additional studies might reveal whether other learners have the same faith in the value of reading as a means to improving their language ability or whether this is a highly idiosyncratic personal theory. Do some of the practices Hamad attributes to school training, such as memorization without understanding, lead learners with a similar training to the same misconceptions and failure to process meaning properly that he initially experienced? A study by Vann and Abraham (1990) on the learning strategies of two unsuccessful Saudi Arabian female learners speculated on the effects of school training in seeking formulaic solutions (similar to the 'cut and paste' approach of Hamad's early school reading practice) to the inability of one learner to process adequately higher-level learning tasks. Is this characteristic of all learners of Hamad's background, and how does it affect their ability to make sense of the information they require for academic success? Further studies of Arabic-speaking learners for whom English is the medium of instruction might help to clarify whether reading strategies that are not particularly helpful persist or are eventually abandoned or revised, as was the case for Hamad.

For language teachers seeking to support their learners' efforts, how can a learner biography like this one help inform their methods? One way might be in reinforcing the caution raised by Horwitz (1987) about the mismatch between a learner's preconceived beliefs and the preferred learning environment of the teacher. As Hamad pointed out, he had had useful instruction on how to read better and faster, but wasn't ready to take it in until his ineffective strategies had led to failure. Nonetheless, even though there was a considerable time lag until he was convinced of the usefulness of what he had been taught, the previous exposure to more effective reading strategies triggered his later course of action, and led him to ask for reassurance and input from a former teacher, although the relationship had now changed to that of guide, rather than dispenser of knowledge. Finally, a biography such as this one may also serve to demonstrate to anxious learners that, while there are no short and simple pathways to becoming an effective language learner, solutions can be found, which are likely to be as individual as the learners themselves.

## Appendix 1: Questions for Hamad

Before the interviews began, Hamad was handed a card containing the following instructions and questions:

Describe your formal English language training (i.e., school, college).

What contact with English did you have outside the classroom? When did it begin? What kind of contact do you have now?

What problems did you face in learning English? Did you overcome them? How?

Describe the most useful, helpful experiences you've had with English language learning.

Have you ever been discouraged? What did you do then?

How helpful have your medical studies been in language learning?

What is your ideal learning situation?

The interviews began as a biography, starting from Hamad's earliest school experiences, but the theme of reading as key emerged fairly quickly after he began to talk about his college English courses, and he frequently sidetracked and returned to it when talking about what seemed to be unrelated matters, such as how his listening improved when he took a course at a private institute.

## Appendix 2: Strategy questionnaire

In addition to answering the questions in Appendix 1, Hamad was asked to complete the Strategy Inventory for Language Learning (Oxford 1990). He stated that he enjoyed doing it, and it is likely that the statements therein also helped him reflect on his previous and current experiences as an English learner as he later reported them in his biography. His overall average score was 3.8, indicating high strategy use. The area he had the highest score in was Compensating for Missing Knowledge, while the lowest was in Remembering More Effectively, but all results were in the High (Usually Used) Strategy Use range.

## Note

1. The data extracts in this chapter are taken from verbatim transcriptions of interviews conducted in English. These extracts have not been edited for grammatical accuracy.

# 7 Learners' constructions of identities and imagined communities

*Tim Murphey, Chen Jin and Chen Li-Chi*

In this paper, we report our preliminary understandings from our qualitative readings of language learning histories (LLHs) written by 84 Japanese and 58 Taiwanese second-semester first-year university students in English. Our focus is on the social construction of learner identities and imagined communities that can nourish learning. We also note moments of dis-identification, lack of imagined community, and times when previously imagined communities change, fade or are forgotten.

The LLHs in the two cultures are consistently irregular. The data is therefore messy and does not allow for a neat quantitative analysis. Having said that, there are patterns that connect (Clarke 2003) the histories together. These patterns are rather remarkable in their portrayal of identity as a factor of difference which teachers can learn from and use to teach more to individual needs. Most of the students report periods of excitement in their learning spurred by particular social encounters with language 'use' mixed with other periods of frustration with educational 'abuse', in which language is often taught just for eventual exams, 'as if we solved mathematics problems' (Yoko JLLH1 p. 5).[1] It is suggested that students might develop more resilience were they to explicitly understand this roller coaster of progress (Murphey 1998e) and their multiple distributed identities in their language learning lives. Teachers could also attend to individual students better after reading their histories, and students themselves could arrive at a general community of explanation through reading each other's LLHs.

Below we first sketch out the theoretical background, briefly describe the contexts in which the histories were written, and then proceed to provide data from the histories to show the dynamic quality of changing identities and imagined communities in the lives of these students. We feel these constructed identities are important differences to be aware of in the classroom as they position students in different socio-emotional positions, provoking different investments in learning. We end with a discussion of some reservations and conclude with a call to allow students fuller participation in their learning by letting them, their identities, their communities and their development be the main subject matter of our courses.

## Background

First-person narratives of language learners have recently been given more attention for the rich information that they might provide concerning the ups and downs and the intricacies of personal investment in language learning (see Norton 2000; Pavlenko and Lantolf 2000; Benson and Nunan 2002; Kinginger and Pavlenko 2002, among others). Research is showing that the social construction in action (Lantolf and Pavlenko 2001) of learners' imagined communities (Norton 2001; Pavlenko and Norton forthcoming) can nourish investments in learning (Norton 2000) and the building of new identities as second language (L2) users (Cook 1999). Lantolf and Pavlenko's (2001) description of sociocultural theory, and more specifically activity theory, below, allows us to see how rich a person's personal history of their learning trajectories and circumstances might be to researchers collecting data on language learning:

> The general theory conceives learners first and foremost as individuals whose formation as thinking and learning beings depends crucially on the concrete circumstances of their specific histories as language learners and as members of the communities of practice to which they belong and to which they aspire. The general theory maintains that human beings develop specifically human ways of behaving (socially, physically, and psychologically) as a consequence of the mediational means (artifacts and social relations) made accessible to them or by them.
>
> (p. 155)

In this chapter we use imagined communities to refer to this social construction of 'communities of practice to which they belong and to which they aspire'. The term 'imagined communities' was used by Anderson (1991) to describe how nation-states use language to provide a sense of community to citizens. These communities are 'imagined' because they are not communities in which everyone actually knows and meets each other. Norton (2001) and Pavlenko and Norton (forthcoming) use 'imagined communities' to describe how language learners are stimulated to invest or not in their language learning depending on the communities that they see, or imagine, themselves belonging to in the present or future. Teachers are in powerful positions to help create such imagined communities and to stimulate or stifle them.

Our contention in this chapter is that students need to have successful experiences of language learning (although data shows that frustrating ones sometimes also work well; see also Block 2002; Skier and Vye 2003) to spark a desire to identify with certain groups and to locate themselves in imagined communities and be seen as successful second language (L2) users (Cook 1999). And, 'because learning transforms who we are and what we can do, it is an experience of identity' (Wenger 1998, p. 215). Unfortunately, language learning activities that posit the native speaker as an ideal model are often in danger of creating dis-identificatory moments of non-participation and marginalization (i.e., leaving slow or lower-level learners out) due to the typically overwhelming distance of the native speaker from many L2 learners. The three concepts of personal identities, imagined communities and investment in learning seem to co-occur or co-construct each other in our understanding: as learners want to belong to a community and construct their identities as members of the group, they invest energy and time into learning how to be like those members.

## Previous pedagogical applications

Murphey's earlier work with Japanese students showed the beneficial aspects of asking students to reflect on their own 'experiences of language learning' by writing their LLHs (Oxford and Green 1996; Murphey 1997). These LLHs were collected and then published in two short collections to be read by fellow students in the same class and in subsequent classes (Murphey 1998a, 1998b). Each person's LLH was seen as uniquely constructed by events, desires, decisions, strategies, beliefs, actions and particular perceptions. Each involved unique trajectories and patterns of investment and de-investment. Writing their histories allowed students to reflect on these forces and to become aware of their own part in making their histories. Ideally this metacognitive awareness allowed them to take more control of future learning, to *own the learning process* they were involved in more completely and to become more self-regulated and autonomous.

Murphey (1999) argued that LLHs are also intensely relevant, level-appropriate narratives for students near the same level to read. They present a variety of strategies, beliefs and attitudes that can be easily modelled because they are written by near peers. Thus, LLHs benefit not only the writers, but also readers, both younger and older. Teachers also can learn how to teach more appropriately from reading their students' LLHs. Junior and senior high school teachers reading collections written by university students can also get insight into students' evaluations of their teaching methods.

## Participants and context

The origins of the 84 Japanese LLHs discussed in this chapter have been outlined above. The 58 Taiwanese LLHs were written in April of 2002. The Japanese and Taiwanese groups were similar in that they were all second-semester first-year students at the time of writing and were being taught by Murphey in an English department in small private universities in their respective countries. The instructions for writing the LLHs, for both groups, were the following:

---

My language learning history

Write a paper about your language learning history from when you began learning English to the present. Length: 3 pages double-spaced (about 750 words). If you like you can send it via e-mail. Some questions you may want to answer in your story:

- How did you learn English in JHS and HS?
- What positive and negative experiences did you have and what did you learn from them?
- What were you expecting before you came to the university?
- What were you surprised about in your university classes?
- How have you changed your ways of language learning since coming to the university?
- What are the things that you found especially helpful?
- What are the areas that you still want to improve in?
- How do you think your next three years will be?
- What are your language learning plans and goals after graduation?
- What advice would you give to next year's first-year students?

Have your paper proofread and signed by two other classmates. Write the following at the end of your paper for their signatures: *I have proofread and given suggestions about this paper.

Signed                    Date:

---

## Data analysis

Excerpts from the LLHs allow us to see degrees of identification or non-identification and investments with imagined communities. Below we briefly quote a total of 32 different students (11 Japanese and 21

Taiwanese) 39 times (14 Japanese and 25 Taiwanese) to ground our observations in their discourse. The fact that we quote more Taiwanese than Japanese is perhaps due to the proximity of the researchers to that group at the time of writing and to fact that their data were more recently collected. The Taiwanese students were also more observable in our everyday lives during the writing of this piece, while the Japanese data were more historical since we were looking at published data from several years earlier. We nevertheless contend that both groups show evidence of the phenomena we describe below and we give examples from each group for each observation.

We first look at the situation in which students report a lack of any imagined community to identify with, which occurred most frequently with initial learning. We then provide data to show how the social construction of imagined communities can occur, using past, present and future orientations. Next, we see how teachers can facilitate moments of identification for students, how students often ride a roller coaster of identifying and dis-identifying, and how friends and near peer role models can be instrumental in the formation of identities and imagined communities. Importantly, we also look at activities leading to de-investing that students report. Finally, evidence of students' own identity constructions as successful L2 users are presented.

### Lack of imagined communities

Many learners seem to start out learning a foreign language, especially in schools, lacking reasons for studying or, in our terms, lacking imagined communities with which to identify and invest their language learning behaviour. In the LLHs, students often initially express feelings of loneliness and of being lost and not knowing why they are learning English.

> In my first English class, I couldn't speak at all with strangers whose speaking was usually better than me. I felt lonely and I wasn't interested in English at all so that I almost gave it up. (Carry TLLH11)

> When I was taking English class, it was like groping in the pitch-dark, and I felt awkward. I think I was lacking in the belief that I could understand even if I tried. (Shuhei JLLH1 p. 9)

> I wondered why we had to learn foreign language in spite of being Japanese. (Yumiko JLLH2 p. 28)

In the worst case students end up fearing or hating English and obviously wanting not to identify themselves with anything having to do with it:

> When I entered high school, I was still not good at English.
> Whenever I was returned my English paper, I trembled. (Shuhei
> JLLH1 p. 9)

> To tell you the truth, it was very hard work and not fun. That is
> why I came to hate English. (Miho JLLH2 p. 22)

> After class, I listened to the cassette for many times in order to
> memorize the sound of the words. It was a difficult job for me to
> do. I did so not because I accepted English but because I didn't
> want to bring shame on myself . . . In short, when it comes to
> English, I was fear to speak and I hate to learn. (Carry TLLH11)

While usually these students did not do well, as Valorie, who wrote, 'I
did not like English because I did not have achievement on it' (Valorie
TLLH5), others were able to get good grades somehow and these good
grades may have motivated them to study, if not to learn:

> Although sometimes I got high grades in high school, I didn't
> really learn English well. (Celin TLLH48)

Rogoff *et al.* (2003) describe how students in schools often have little or
no 'intent participation', i.e., the intention to actually use what they are
learning, because they are separated from the mature activities in which
such information and skills are actually used. Being able to imagine a
community in which we might belong and use the information we are
learning would seem to provide such participation with intent.

### The social construction of imagined communities

We would like to propose that students might imagine communities in
at least three ways. They may imagine 'present communities' that exist
in the here and now and motivate them in a similar way to Anderson's
(1991) citizens imagining a nation-state of like-minded patriots. Students
might also project into the future and imagine a more distant community to which they hope some day to belong. Then there is the possibility of remembering past imagined communities and comparing them
with the present as many do below. Future research needs to tease out
the differences between these kinds of imagined communities and how
they work to stimulate learning in students. Below we provide examples
of two types of imagined communities which emerged from the data with
some brief commentary.

### The past's future imagination updated by the present

Students often reported that they had imagined college life (future orientation) differently before actually coming to the university. This is

perhaps to be expected since they were imagining things they had never experienced. Some students were disappointed in some aspects, some challenged, some pleasantly surprised and some had a mixture of all of these as they updated these past conceptions in the present.

> In my imagination of college life, we would carry thick and heavy English classical novels, going from classroom to classroom, and have great pressure. However, to my surprise, we usually learn this language here by storytelling, playing games, or other kinds of activities.(Sara TLLH8)

> Before I came here, I was expecting to have classes with foreign students. Now I do not feel my English is useful so much. I want to acquire much more practical knowledge of English as soon as possible. (Michiko JLLH1 p. 15)

Their present descriptions, however, sometimes imply that they think their present community is more or less the same for most university students, or at least other students in the same university.

> And I think [thought] the classes in college must very serious. But when I attended university, I found the classes are more interesting than before. We can learn English by many different ways and most of them are fun. I really enjoy learning in college classes and have many unforgettable experiences. (Polly TLLH31)

The quote below shows not only how past imagined communities are updated, but also how teachers' encouraging self-regulation in the selection of learning means and strategies can provide identifying moments of agency to students. We will return later to the discussion of self-regulation below.

> I was expecting colorful life before I came to the university. In my imagination, I can learn what I want to learn and I can take participate in many clubs to enrich my life. But true life was not as the same as my imagination. At first, I was surprised about my classmates' speaking and listening. Afterwards, I was [surprised] about to know the way we can learn English we didn't have to learn English unwillingly but we could choose the way I liked to learn and learned much more. Therefore, I couldn't be free until I was the boss to decide what I wanted and I just did it. (Carry TLLH1)

## Future communities

In the comments below we see how students wish to join communities spurred by wanting to understand the characters in Disney cartoons,[2] wanting to be a translator, or to be like their teacher and travel.

> At the time I was 11 years old and one day I asked my father if he could let me go to the English cram school for children. The reason was that I liked to see the Disney cartoon. . . . I thought that the pronunciation of English was very beautiful. Therefore I had a strong desire to learn English as soon as possible. (Mary TLLH55)

Below, Carry not only imagines a future community, but takes actions to step into the shoes of its members. This imagining that 'I am one of them' can be an effective learning strategy for some learners. However, the fact is that for most language learners there are not enough native speakers around to emulate most of the time. Unknowingly, such students may also be going through a lot of stress trying to attain the native-speaker standard.[3]

> It was worthy of note that I sometimes pretended to be a foreigner and read loudly articles. Under my deep soul, there was a dream to be an interpreter with wonderful accent and fluent English. (Carry TLLH11)

Below, Hiromi's modelling of her teacher would appear to be more ecological with proximal goals than Carry's modelling of native speakers. Much also depends on the availability of models. Hiromi is modelling more of a near peer role model (discussed more below) and partially for non-language reasons (travel) which are more easily attained than 'native-speaker mastery'.

> I started studying English at a private school, and I dreamed to be like my teacher because she told me many interesting stories which she had experienced in foreign countries. (Hiromi JLLH2 p. 26)

### Desire to join a non-native teacher's community

In many of the LLHs, as in the last quote above, students mentioned 'a good teacher' as inspiring them to want to learn and to belong to a community of English speakers. It is worthy of note that often liking their teachers, and building a respectful rapport with them, spurs many students to imagine such communities and to accept challenges that they might not otherwise consider.

> At first, I did not like English very much. But I liked our English teacher. I wanted to be praised by him so I was enthusiastic in the class. (Yoshiko JLLH2 p. 16)

> I considered me push by my teacher very much. Sometimes I felt a little nervous to attend her class maybe she thought that I could do much better than what I did at that time. She told us that learning

a new language needed perseverance and interests. I was moved by her words and I became to admire her so much. (Ellen TLLHS4)

Teachers need to realize the power that they have to present imagined communities or to be model members of imagined communities of L2 users for their students. One can easily imagine that if one does not like the teacher, the subject taught by the teacher will most likely produce the same emotions, especially one so tied to identity as to come out of our mouths. We can almost hear students say, 'I do not want to sound like Mr X, I don't like him.' Teachers who inspire develop their students' imagination and stimulate their investment in creating an L2 identity that can greatly facilitate their learning. They do this through first being good models of the community of L2 users themselves. Even native-speaker teachers can become near peer role models of L2 learning when students see them studying other languages.

### Riding the roller coaster

Our imagined communities sometimes do not work out to be what we expect them to be. We can often feel like we are on a virtual roller coaster of emotions, mixed motivations and desires (Murphey 1998e).

> When I was a junior high school student, I did not like English very much . . . In English class, we only read the textbook, picked up some grammatically important things and did workbooks repeatedly. The teacher did not speak English nor did they let us listen to tapes in their classes. (Yoko JLLH1 p. 5)

This lacklustre beginning to Yoko's English learning changed when she met an exchange student later who stayed at her house for three weeks. However, it was the frustration she felt with her inability to communicate that spurred her on to learn English:

> Sometimes I tried to speak to him but I could not because my brother was good at speaking English and I did not want to be compared with him. Moreover when he talked to me, I could not catch what he said at all, and it was at the time that I decided to study English and to talk with him one day. (Yoko JLLH1 p. 5)

Yoko's imagined community began with this boy and entailed wishing she could perform as her brother did. Her brother was a near peer role model (Murphey and Arao 2001) who had access to this imagined community that she did not. However her investment (Norton 2000) faded later: 'But in high school I forgot the original purpose of learning English (to speak) and studied only grammar again.' In university, Yoko became excited once again with her studies. This roller coaster of Yoko's investment can be seen through the social situations in which she was stimulated to create imagined communities and identify positively with learning. The LLHs show how students can invest themselves in language learning but that these investments can fade and change with the imagined communities and the desires to identify with them. Near peer role models that are available to them in proximity and frequency are instrumental in feeding these new identities.

### The impact of making friends and near peer role modelling

Two facilitators of creating imagined communities seem to be the making of friends (Murphey 1998c) and the targeting of near peer role models (Murphey 1998d), which can be one and the same (Murphey and Arao 2001). Being allowed and encouraged to make friends among classmates can create a real-time learning community that thrives on its own energy.

> I am really glad that I could meet lots of friends from different parts of Taiwan but all with the same enthusiasm and interest toward English. I have gained lots experiences of learning English from my classmates, my roommates, and of course my partners. (Trudy TLLH10)

The three citations below show that when a class can have sustained collaborative interaction, imagined communities overlap with actual classes in real time through near peer role modelling.

> I didn't know my classmates could teach me vocabulary until entering college . . . The greatest progress I made after entering college was that I was not afraid to speak English anymore . . . These were impossible before I entered college. (Lance TLLH50)

> To learn with partners is very helpful. To speak, to discuss, and to ask each other questions with classmates or roommates can make learning more lively and interesting. Also, to know some studying tips and to really use them in order to make learning more efficient and easier to remember is helpful. (Annili TLLH2)

> [in university] it is also helpful to have a good partner when learning a language. I didn't have such strong feelings before entering university, but through the interaction with my classmates in class for several times, I can see the effects on me. It is efficient and fast to learn from each other. For example, I can learn some new vocabulary from my partner, I can learn how to say better English sentences by shadowing what my partner says, and I can ask my partner to speak English with me when walking in the campus . . . etc. There too many advantages to having a good partner. (Mary TLLH55)

Near peer role modelling, in which a student feels a desire to become like another person who is already 'near' in many ways (ethnicity, interests, sex, age, frequency of contact, etc.), occurred often in the LLHs. Most often, students cited teachers before university ('Because I wanted to be like her, I did every homework she gave me'; Ayako JLLH2 p. 29) and peers after university (Yamashita 1998). This is probably due to the non-interactive pedagogy predominantly found in exam preparation systems for universities. Since most students don't interact with each other in English in junior and senior high schools, they are simply not available to be models for each other. The more interactive instruction used in many university settings, as shown in the above citations, lends itself to the formation of more friendships, more modelling and a greater sense of a supportive community. The quote below is an example of a near peer role model outside of the school context.

> When I was a 4 class student, my cousin came from Brazil and she can speak English very fluently. I really envy her. From then on, I encourage myself to major in English when enter college. And maybe one day I can speak English well like her. (Polly TLLH32)

Finally, Yukari, below, tells how she learned English when she was abroad in the USA for several years mainly through her peers:

> I also learned a lot of English through daily life with friends and from studying at school. Not only English but other things as well. Probably my friends were my best teachers of English. (Yukari JLLH1 p. 45).

### Activities leading to de-investing and dis-identifying

As noted already while discussing the roller coaster above, investments in identifying can fade or change rapidly and then return again. In the LLHs, de-investing is most often reported in connection to changes in pedagogy, most often with an overemphasis on grammar teaching, as the two citations below show:

> In JHS, I learned only grammar and how to read for almost all of the class. So I did not have a chance to have a conversation with friends in English. (Yukiyo JLLH2 p. 19)

> In HS teachers taught us only grammar. They even used Japanese in English class. I was not satisfied with the classes. (Tomoko JLLH2 p. 25)

The grammar teaching was mainly connected to exams that were frequently cited as the cause for de-investment.

[the] next year, I started to study for the entrance exam. The class became boring again. (Hiroshi JLLH1 p. 31)

It's a form here [Taiwan] that we students study only for tests and not looking for a wider horizon, which I think somehow it has slowed my learning on English for I wasn't really learning anything. (Sharon TLLH34).

One further area that causes de-investment was the lack of respect or sensitivity felt by the student from the teacher, perhaps often unintentionally, as in this citation:

One day I only got 20 points in my test. Then the teacher saw my paper and said 'Polly, congratulation!' That's really broke my heart, though I knew the teacher just made a joke, I still felt upset that time. (Polly TLLH19)

While there may be many reasons students de-invest in learning, there are also ample reasons for investing. Investing in language learning is usually spurred by a significant event involving the creation of an imagined community, often with near peer role models and friends. These are the topic of the next section.

### Identities as successful L2 users

'Success breeds success' because it creates identities and self-efficacy beliefs about whatever skills are being used. However, for many students success in the classroom would appear as rare as a riot in a nunnery. Classrooms, too often, are places where teachers are looking for mistakes rather than successes, as if they were quality control managers in a factory. Thus, in many of the LLHs the startlingly clear success episodes, what Block (2002) refers to as 'crucial experiences', often happen outside the classroom. Lore's ability was confirmed (below) by his interlocutor, by a stranger on a bus (What if God was one of us?), who had no investment in evaluating him as a successful L2 user (Cook 1999). Perhaps more than making Lore like English, the stranger made Lore like himself and then see himself as a successful L2 user. Such critical incidents can create great investments in learning.

When I took bus home, I met a foreigner and I come to him and spoke with him in English for a little while, although I knew my English was poor, that man encouraged and said, 'You have great English.' I was happy. When I got home I was grateful for him because he gave something I wanted for a long time. He made me like English. (Lore TLLH15).

The construction of identities as successful L2 users can happen in the classroom only if students actually are successful using English meaningfully, i.e., for real purposes, *in the classroom*. We contend that such moments of identifying themselves as L2 users will happen more often when they find themselves in appropriately interactive classes, as suggested in the student citations below:

> The biggest different in my language learning since coming to the university was that I had more chances to speak English. When I studied in junior and senior high, I focused on grammar. Now, I speak English everyday and try my best to read plenty of English books. (Angie TLLH17)

> I feel I am in a fortunate environment. I have OC [oral communication] classes three times a week. And thanks to LL tapes, my listening ability has improved little by little. In this university, there are many foreigners and role models. My classmates are diligent to be good English speakers. Their eager attitude makes me want to improve more. (Rie JLLH2 p. 10)

Setting incrementally increasing percentage goals for English use in classes and reflecting in action logs (Murphey 1993) can help students develop their reflection literacy (Hasan 1996).

> Now, I almost speak 100% English class, and have a lot of chances to speak English, such as when I chat with friends. In that way my oral comprehension got improved naturally. (Fred TLLH44)

Schunk and Zimmerman (1997, p. 39) argue that 'achievement research shows that goals do not automatically enhance learning and motivation'; rather, 'the goal properties of specificity, proximity, and difficulty are important'. Encouraging students to set their own goals regularly and to know their peers' goals through intensive interaction brings specificity and proximity to their efforts, making success more likely. Students confirmed this in their descriptions of intensive interaction in the classes.

> Before, I considered all classes as boring. After entering university, I found how colorful and fresh. We have many chances to express our opinions and we have the right to learn what we would like to learn. (Lorry TLLH13)

> Besides Extensive Reading, I have found that Extensive Speaking also helps our learning. (Joan TLLH58)

> The greatest progress I made after entering college was that I was not afraid to speak English anymore. (Lance TLLH50)

Catherine, below, attributes the increase in English to the teacher and perhaps is in a transition stage of realizing that it really is her choice to use English and identify with it, rather than just having an encouraging teacher. She is on her way to owning her own success.

> I am surprised about how much English we are speaking in your class. Every class with you seems like to be noisier than the Taiwanese traditional market. You have taught us to be very talkative in and out of the class – in English!! You encourage us to talk, and you have made us feel that it's a proud thing to do to speak English. (Catherine TLLH7)

## Constructing identities through writing LLHs

The act of composing one's LLH can have its own effects on identity building and the positioning of students in relationship to their language learning and this, too, needs further study. In writing their LLHs, the roller coaster of their language learning becomes clearer to them; they become more conscious of what contributes to their learning and what inhibits it. Several students commented on these points at a meta-discursive level:

> I have studied English for seven years. My way of studying was not effective until I entered the university. My way of thinking sometimes prevented me from speaking English. It must be helpful for my studying hereafter to look back on my language learning history. (Yoko JLLH1 p. 5)

> Before I start introducing my English language learning history, I want to tell you it is certainly helpful for me to understand what I have learned in English since beginning to get in touch with it and what my goals and my plans are in the future. If you don't assign this homework I will never think these important things about myself. It is surely a great chance for me to know my attitude for English. (Melanie TLLH10)

Constructing and reconstructing our LLHs can be an act of confirming and realizing the extent to which we are already an L2 user, making it stronger and more resilient, which can give us confidence and the desire to develop it even further. As Schunk and Zimmerman (1997, p. 47) note:

> It is important to develop a resilient sense of self-efficacy in students as competent readers and writers [and speakers]. There is substantial evidence indicating that students' efficacy beliefs can be enhanced by social interventions such as modeled use of strategies and feedback emphasizing learning progress and by deliberate self-regulatory efforts involving goal setting and self-evaluation.

We contend that writing the LLHs invited 'deliberate self-regulatory efforts involving goal setting and self-evaluation'. However, we question whether this would be the case with students who had not yet experienced a variety of ways to learn. Without sufficient experience in contrasting conditions, the histories would probably be less exciting, the roller coasters would be more flat, or they would simply reinforce the status quo of entrance exam oriented teaching. We would predict that this would have happened with the present groups had they simply written the LLHs immediately upon entering university, before they had had much experience of difference. While students are individually different, they also need enough time in different situated learning communities for perceptions of difference, of self and learning means, to sink in. Thus, the timing of the writing of LLHs in the second semester of university, rather than the first, may account for these students' greater awareness of the differences in the ways of teaching and learning.

## Discussion

These students all wrote these short LLHs as a class assignment with the teacher (first author) as the main audience and with guidelines. This same teacher was also teaching them several times a week and for many students he was the first native speaker they had contact with. Thus, the construction of their stories in English for a teacher figure may certainly reflect these features. As researchers we might ask, 'How might the LLHs have been different if done in their L1 and for another audience?' While some students may have been at times disturbed by the target reader, we contend that the strength of the narrative turn, the power of personally telling your own story, empowered writers to express and construct their stories honestly as they saw them, from their points of view, most of the time.

We also contend that writing their LLHs made many students more reflective and metacognitive about their learning. They were not simply reporting their experience of learning as it was subjectively and partially remembered at that point in time but constructing an understanding of it by thinking through the different learning trajectories that they had taken and through re-reading what they were writing. Research on writing shows us that we discover things as we write and do not always know what is going to come next. Research on how our memories work also tells us that we do not remember things exactly as they were but that things are forgotten, enlarged, and transformed at least somewhat over time. However, this subjective material is still important because it is these transformed memories that we use to remember who we are/were and what we do/did, to decide what we believe and to form an approximate appraisal of who we are now.

Furthermore, writing their LLHs in English perhaps allowed the students to invest (Norton 2000) more in their learning through the firmer constructions of their English user identities. Students are not merely reporting past learning experiences, rather the act of writing LLHs both constructs and gives impetus to learning through establishing who we might be in certain particular situations – for these students, first-year university English majors.

Students' reading a group of their peers' LLHs, as these and later students did, can also have an impact on identity-building. When a variety of peer LLHs are read together they serve as sociocultural tools for navigating one's future paths, as well as understanding one's past, as readers compare and contrast their own experiences, identify similar conflicts and successes and appropriate strategies, beliefs and attitudes that they see as desirable. Because of the strong similarity of the learning paths in these groups of LLHs, the writers are strong near peer role models that make for facile emulation of specific and proximal goals. At the same time there is variety in how they go about constructing their identities which refreshingly offers many choices for ways to be in the world (Gee 1996).

Also through reading each other's LLHs, these students develop as a community of explanation and of practice (Freeman 1994) as they describe and explain how they weathered the years of English instruction and struggles with the entrance exams. Their 'imagined community' comes alive the more they read examples of other students, like themselves, failing and succeeding. The closer the readers are to the writers in age, ethnicity and situational constraints, the more easily they will identify with the experiences and the more impact the stories will have. While the first author has been able to observe these things in his classes, it deserves more investigation with pre- and post-course questionnaires.

## Conclusion

We suggest that the act of writing one's LLH is a social construction that takes as its main topic our dynamically 'distributed identities' that are multiple, conflicted and still changing and yet, in the metacognitive act of composition, become firmer and stronger. Identities are multiple as we trace the course of our many ways of being in the world (Gee 1996) in the past and present and note how they match and conflict with each other and our imagined communities. This 'distributed subjectivity' (Claire Kramsch's preferred term, personal communication) changes in degrees over time and space depending on who we interact with, where and when, and our acts of cognition. We both construct and are constructed by others' subjectivities as we share agency inter-mentally within activity systems (Wertsch, Tulviste and Hagstrom 1993), that is, we read others' LLHs and construct our own. If the unit of analysis for understanding learning is 'the person and the mediational means' (ibid.), then LLHs would seem to have special importance as they are reflections about mediational means (ways of learning). Furthermore, the act of writing about one's LLH enables students to develop more agency, more self-regulation in their lives, as they become more cognizant of the mediational means that account for their trajectories. To the extent that the LLHs allow this, they are a meta-mediational means. Thus, an activity system, i.e., a class, can potentially become more emancipatory through having as the primary subject matter the participants, their stories, their identies and their development.

In Bateson's (1994, p. 41) words, 'participation precedes learning'. We might ask ourselves if students are too often being held back on the periphery of learning too long, with vague L2 identities, by teachers teaching too much and not allowing students to participate in their learning more fully (Lave and Wenger 1991). Through writing and talking about who they have been in their different learning situations and who they are (or want to be) now in the present one, students themselves become the topic of the class, and teachers have more information as to how they can adjust their pedagogy to make it truly student-centred (Murphey and Woo 1998). Providing space for clarifying and constructing identities when done in the target language also encourages identifying with the language as a means of self-construction, a way to explore and construct 'the person and the mediational means'.

## Notes

1. Citations from the Japanese corpus (JLLH) are from the published editions and have been corrected somewhat and the names and page numbers are consistent with these editions. Citations taken from the Taiwanese corpus (TLLH) have not been corrected or published yet and the names are pseudonyms. Numbers are used for research tracking.
2. Watching television can be a non-threatening experience and, if we are watching characters that we have already become attached to and even films (cartoons) that we have already seen, there is a certain familiarity that can draw us in. Watching an old Mel Gibson movie in Italy recently, dubbed in Italian, Murphey had the impression of belonging to those people who speak Italian, and Italian became much more familiar to him (psychologically), and he was telling himself secretly that he could easily learn Italian. This is a nontrivial process that can spur a lot of initial identification among learners and facilitate learning.

3. Research is also showing us how trying to be too much like the native speaker can be frustrating for many students and that it would be better to point students towards the goal of becoming competent L2 users (Cook 1999). Still, I have met a few learners who have insisted that the native speaker is their goal. Whether this has been drummed into them by other teachers or it is simply their belief, to their credit they usually have sustained a very high degree of motivation to learn because of it.

.

# 8   'It's just rules . . . that's all it is at this stage . . .'

*Sara Cotterall*

Many learners who wish to learn a language choose to enrol in a formal course. Their subsequent experience generally involves some degree of compromise between their agendas and those of their teachers. So, how exactly does the negotiation of learner and teacher agendas occur? To what extent is it possible for the learner to subvert the teacher's agenda, or for the teacher to take account of the learner's agenda? These and other related questions prompted me to take advantage of the opportunity to track an adult student as he participated in a first-year Spanish course at university. The goal of the project was to explore the learner's goals and beliefs about language learning as part of his ongoing experience of learning the language during a 12-week course. My interest lay, in particular, in the extent to which the learner assumed control of his learning process.

Therefore this chapter documents, largely in his own words, a student's experience of participating in a beginner-level language course at university. The learner repeatedly compares his study of Spanish with his experience of studying other subjects at university, and reflects on the social context in which his learning takes place. No claims for the representativeness of this account are made. On the contrary, I argue that the only way in which a collective and comprehensive understanding of learners' experiences of taught courses can be gained is by accumulating a significant number of individual accounts.

## Previous research

A number of accounts of individual learners' experiences of learning a language have appeared in the research literature. These include both first-person accounts, such as those found in Bailey (1983), Schmidt and Frota (1986), Jones (1994) and Belcher and Connor (2001), and also biographical accounts, where the reporter of the experience is a researcher with privileged access to the learner, either through interviews, diary entries or some other means. This chapter falls into the second category. One early example of a biographical study of a learner was Schmidt's (1983) account of the naturalistic experience of 'Wes' learning English as a second language in Hawaii. A completely different approach is adopted by Evans (1988), who seeks to present a picture of the discipline of modern languages teaching and learning in the United Kingdom based on interviews with 50 students and 50 staff. While Evans' aim is achieved by presenting the voices of individual learners and teachers, ultimately his focus is on profiling the discipline as a whole, rather than on the experience of individual learners.

A much more detailed picture of individual learner histories is presented in Norton's (2000) longitudinal case study of five immigrant women learning French in Canada. Her data are based on both the subjects' formal language learning and their experiences of acquiring the target language after formal instruction had finished. Norton is primarily concerned with interactions between native speakers and non-native speakers of the target language, and the social context in which these interactions occur. Accordingly, she maintains the importance (in second language acquisition contexts) of paying attention to relations of power between language learners and target language speakers in order to understand individuals' language learning trajectories fully. Her case studies illustrate how the life and work contexts of her case subjects had profound effects on their willingness and opportunities to interact with members of the target language community. To see the act of language learning in isolation from this context, she claims, is to see only part of the picture.

Learners' perceptions of classroom learning in foreign language settings have also been investigated by researchers. Slimani (1989, 1992) obtained learner reports on uptake, which she defined as 'what learners claim to have learned at the end of a lesson' (Slimani 1989, p. 223). She asked 13 Algerian first-year university students to complete an 'uptake recall chart' at the end of six lessons which she observed and tape-recorded. Analysis of her data revealed that items initiated by fellow learners were more likely to be identified as 'uptake' by learners than were items initiated by the teacher. Furthermore, a learner who initiated a topic was less likely to report that item as having been learned, than his or her classmates. Slimani's studies provide some tentative evidence for the priority of learner agendas over teacher agendas.

Block (1994) also focused on the micro level of classroom activity, exploring the different perceptions of 12 learners, their teacher and an observer of a day's tasks in an English class in Barcelona. Block shows how the learners and the teacher had quite different views on the purpose and salience of particular tasks. Block (1996a, p. 171) reports on a study in which six MBA candidates who were participating in a compulsory English course and their English teacher kept an oral diary 'reporting on what they thought was going on in class on a day-to-day basis' for a period of one month. Once again, Block found considerable variation in the accounts, particularly between teacher and individual learner perceptions. He devotes the second part of his article to a detailed discussion of the reactions of one student, and to an examination of the extent to which his diary entries (which were highly detailed and analytic) paralleled or diverged from those of the teacher. Block concludes that the learners in the study were often unclear of the purpose of the tasks they were asked to perform in class, and as a result felt that they were wasting their time in class. These studies provide substantial evidence of learner 'agendas' which are at odds with those of their teachers.

A longitudinal approach to narrating one classroom learner's experience is adopted by Swain and Miccoli (1994), who tracked an adult ESL student enrolled in a graduate course in Education over a university term. The course in which the learner was enrolled – entitled 'Collaborative learning in second language classrooms' – required her to participate in group work in every session, and to participate in a collaborative research project in the second part of the course. A number of group work sessions in which the case subject took part were video- and audio-taped, with one of the authors observing and taking field notes. These field notes were later used in generating questions to ask the subject during interview sessions. The group-work method was neither familiar nor comfortable for the learner. The article highlights the salient role played by the learner's feelings and beliefs in her classroom experiences. Indeed, the authors argue that the learner's 'conscious reflection about her negative emotions and their sources allowed her to act on them, resulting in enhanced second language learning' (Swain and Miccoli 1994, p. 15). In this way, the research methodology may have contributed positively to the learning outcomes of the course.

Block (1998) also adopts a longitudinal approach in documenting an adult language learner's efforts to learn English at a language school in Barcelona during the course of a trimester. Block's goal in interviewing the learner was to obtain his dynamic and evolving evaluation of the language course in which he was enrolled. This was part of the author's attempt to question the validity of a 'simple pen-and-paper, end-of-course evaluation form based on a one-to-five number scale'. Block concluded that his subject's complex reactions to the unfolding course could not be adequately captured by any formal objective evaluation form. He comments in particular on the ambivalence of many of his informant's comments. In this paper, he also commented on his previous research, saying:

> This research showed me that while learners might agree in general on what they do during lessons on a day-to-day basis and even why they are doing it, for the most part they tend to focus on their own individual concerns when providing accounts.
>
> (Block 1998, p. 150)

The most striking difference between the learner perceptions Block reports on in his articles (Block 1994, 1996a, 1998) and the commentary provided by the informant in this chapter is the object of focus. While Block's informants report in great detail on the minute-by-minute tasks of their language classes, the subject reported on in this chapter is primarily concerned with fitting language learning (as it is constructed in his course) into his broader perspective of learning and into his life.

The type of university context in which this chapter's subject was learning a language is considered by some to be a hostile setting for the fostering of learner autonomy, or the incorporation of learner agendas. Hurd (1998, p. 72) comments:

> realistically, only a partial autonomy can be exercised by students in a university context, precisely because the goals and objectives are already in place before a student enrols.

While this is undoubtedly true, it is important to seek insights into how learners make sense of the curriculum. The outcome of such research is likely to be an enhanced understanding of the range of agendas which learners bring to their language courses, and the way in which learner and course agendas interact.

## Research methodology

The case study presented in this chapter conceived of the subject as research partner in the exploration of his experience of the language course. The interviews were highly interactive, with the subject leading much of the discussion, following an initial prompt by the author at the start of each session. Six interviews were held over a four-month period, with the interviewer asking open-ended questions at the beginning of each session and encouraging the learner to raise issues or topics which were salient to him from that week's classes. All interviews were audio-taped and later transcribed. Once the interviews were over and the data analysed, the author sent a copy of the draft account to the subject for comment. The informant agreed that the article reflected his experience of the course and contributed a number of comments on his experience of participating in the research project (some of which are included in this paper).

In this chapter, the interview data are treated as 'a product of the interaction between interviewer and interviewee' (Block 2000, p. 759), acknowledging the extent to which interviews are 'co-constructed discourse events'. Consequently, the interview data are deliberately presented, as far as is possible, in the learner's own words. According to Block (2000, p. 759):

> The conceptualization of interviews as co-constructions means that interview data are seen not as reflections of underlying memory but as *voices* adopted by research participants in response to the researcher's prompts and questions. These voices might or might not truly represent what the research participant thinks or would choose to say in another context and on another occasion.

Block summarizes his view of the dynamics of research interviews by presenting a diagram, which depicts a continuum on which different perceptions of interview data can be located. The methodological approach adopted in examining the interview data reported on here tends towards the symptomatic (as opposed to veridical), presentational (as opposed to representational), social, interactive and co-constructed ends of Block's continuum.

## Context

The subject, Harry,[1] was recruited for the research project following the author's visit to a first-year Spanish class in the second week of the first trimester of 1999. Harry was selected as a research subject (together with two other students) on the basis of his availability at times convenient to the researcher. He was a 29-year-old native speaker of English enrolled in his first year of study towards a Bachelor of Arts degree at Victoria University of Wellington. In addition to Spanish, Harry was enrolled in courses in English medieval poetry, French, and religious studies. His previous language learning experience included a year of French at secondary school, and a brief period spent living in Spain with his brother, a fluent speaker of Spanish.

At 29, Harry was a little older than the majority of first-year students, since he had trained as a chef on leaving school and worked in this profession for a number of years. Harry explained that his decision to enrol at university and in a Spanish course was part of a plan to 'get my brain functioning I'm really interested in languages I'm really interested in writing and words words are I love words' (1/7.00). A few years previously, Harry reported, he had taken stock of his life and decided, 'there was nothing that I have ever done that I really thought that I wanted to do as far as a career was concerned'. Enrolling at university was therefore part of a plan to acquire new skills and knowledge which might suggest a new direction in his life.

The Spanish course in which Harry was enrolled was a 12-week (one trimester) introductory course. It involved five hours of class contact per week: three one-hour language classes (lecture format), one audio-visual class and one oral tutorial. The course outline identified the course aims as being to 'introduce students to the basics of the language through practice in speaking, listening, reading and writing'. The course objectives were stated in the following terms:

> Upon completing the course successfully you will be able to:
>
> - understand simple spoken Spanish;
> - relate Spanish sounds to their written forms;
> - pronounce a simple Spanish text with a fair degree of accuracy and fluency;
> - demonstrate a knowledge of basic Spanish grammar;
> - write simple sentences about yourself, using present and past tenses and a basic vocabulary;
> - demonstrate knowledge of the Spanish language appropriate to a variety of everyday situations;
> - translate and answer questions on simple Spanish texts.
>
> (SPAN 111 course outline, 1999)

Harry and I met in my office once every two weeks from March to June 1999 throughout the 12-week trimester. At the time of the first interview, Harry's course was in its second week. In the first session, I explained the objectives of the research, outlined the format of the sessions, and obtained written consent for the sessions to be audio-recorded (and transcribed) and the material used (anonymously) for research purposes. Each session lasted approximately one hour, after which an appointment for the next session was made. Harry participated in six interview sessions in total.

Block (1995b) identifies four social constraints which operate in exchanges between researchers and informant interviewees: the social construction of the interviewee, power imbalances, performing and the nature of the discourse processes. While each of these constraints is acknowledged as having played a role in the current study, the informant's confident, open nature and the rapport that we established helped reduce the normal distorting effects of these constraints. In an attempt to validate the perspective documented here, I sought feedback from Harry on a draft of this chapter and was reassured by the following comment:

> as an interviewer . . . you made me feel absolutely comfortable. Apart from anything else, you became the person upon whom I unloaded my anxieties, and with whom I shared my triumphs, re my Spanish. In that light then, it is easy to understand why things seemed to flow with great fluidity.
>
> (Harry, personal communication, 29 July 2002)

This account of Harry's language learning has been organized around three main themes which emerged from the transcripts. Within each theme, material is presented chronologically – since changes in the learner's perceptions over time are of ultimate importance. The key themes which emerged from the interview data were: the gradual narrowing of the learner's goals, the learner's fluctuating affective state and his changing conceptualizations of the nature of language learning. Each of these themes is explored in what follows.

## Goals and motivation

Harry's goals in enrolling in the Spanish course fitted into his broader motivation for enrolling at university. In explaining his decision to enrol at university as a 'mature student', Harry reported: 'this is a year to prove something. I really just want to get as much out of it as I can' (1/12.00). In one of the interviews Harry made the point that he had made a deliberate decision to give up his job and pay substantial fees in order to study, suggesting a high level of commitment and motivation. This was in contrast to his experience of enrolling at university several years earlier (1/7.00):

> I mucked around at Otago University a couple of y- about s- five or six seven years ago achieved very little arrived there with a hangover and . . . ended up just having a lot of fun and going to heaps of parties and . . . virtually did nothing.

A number of different motives contributed to Harry's decision to include a Spanish paper in his first year at university. Firstly, Harry saw the study of Spanish as linked to his interest in English literature and language:

> I kind of thought French and Spanish . . . having these associations with the English that we speak today . . . I don't know there is a tie there and I just kind of thought this this medieval poetry number it kind of starts at about the thirteenth century and moves up to sort of the time of Shakespeare and . . . I thought that would be quite an interesting sort of thing to slot in there next to it all and it kind of . . . there are little bits that sort of feed all three including the English that we speak now . . . (1/1.00)

Harry also indicated that visiting his brother in Spain several years earlier had contributed to his desire to learn Spanish. When prompted to specify his Spanish-related goals in more detail, Harry (1/15.00) stated that he wanted to go to Spain and be able to talk to people in the street one day, as part of his personal '10-year plan'. At the end of the first interview session, he explained:

> South America is . . . at arm's length . . . I'm afraid to go there . . . that's where I want to live that's where I want to go there and stay

> there you know but I'm just holding it off for now and just keeping it at bay but I'll certainly I want to get there and stay there for a long long time. (1/32.00)

In discussing his travel-associated motivation, Harry explained that he liked to 'fit in' when he was in a foreign country, elaborating as follows:

> I don't want to go to a place like Spain and have people think, oh he's not Spanish . . . I'd like to be as Spanish as I can possibly be . . . when in Rome, do as the Romans . . . (1/29.00)

A further motivation for Harry's decision to learn Spanish was his wider interest in the Hispanic world:

> Just the exposure to all aspects of the Hispanic . . . region is kind of where I'm thinking . . . I just happen to be concentrating solely on the language, but I want to get the movie thing, the people thing, the art thing . . . you know, all that sort of stuff . . . fashion and you know music . . . I want to . . . it's all part of the picture for me. (2/13.00)

It would appear, therefore, that Harry's language learning goals were significantly broader and considerably more ambitious than the course goals of introducing students to 'the basics of the language'.

As evidence of his positive motivation towards learning the language, Harry explained in the first interview that he had become involved in the university's Spanish Club:

> We all sort of got together like and . . . last night was great . . . it was the first meeting and thirty-seven people turned up and paid up and it was you know it was five bucks and we watched a film . . . we talked away and there were people from all different backgrounds . . . I walked home talking all the Spanish words that I knew you know . . . it's kind of cool. (1/14.00)

It later emerged that Harry had been elected president of the Spanish Club, a role that he maintained throughout the trimester but which caused him some frustration, as will be reported in the next section. His participation in the Spanish Club and his enthusiasm for organizing social functions through the club were testimony to his integrative motivation.

As far as the course itself was concerned, Harry reported that the lectures were the most motivating component:

> I like . . . the lecture because we've got (lecturer's name) the man with his you know . . . it's not just what he says coming out of his mouth but how he says it you know and it's this whole thing of moving his arms and expressing himself with his body as well and his posture and his . . . you know . . . I think's an important part of learning a language you've got to understand the delivery as well as the content.

The lecturer concerned was in fact a native speaker of Italian who had a native-like command of Spanish and taught both Italian and Spanish language courses at the university.

Harry also displayed awareness of factors likely to feed his motivation to persist with the course. One of these was his desire for contact with a native speaker; he hoped that by meeting with a native speaker he would be able to use what he had learned of the language. Several weeks into the course, I was able to introduce Harry to a student from Spain whom he arranged to meet for conversation practice. In the fourth interview, Harry commented that meeting the native speaker outside of class was 'essential . . . need it to keep me interested' (4/28.00).

However, as the weeks passed, Harry's goals narrowed dramatically. In the fifth session (during Week 10 of the 12-week course), he identified his goal as being simply to pass the course:

> My goal . . . my focus now is not to give up and say oh stuff it I've failed this paper . . . my goal now is to draw still as much from this paper as I possibly can. (5/26.00)

This kind of pragmatic orientation was, in fact, relatively commonly observed amongst the foreign language learners who attended the Language Advisory Service. Despite this disappointing conclusion to his first experience of Spanish at university, in the final interview Harry professed an ongoing commitment to the language, reporting that he intended to remain involved in the Spanish Club (6/7.00) although he had decided to cancel his enrolment in the second trimester Spanish course (6/18.00). His decision not to continue with Spanish at university seemed to be based on his perception that Spanish required a type of learning and a time commitment which he was not prepared to make:

> In giving the second Spanish paper away I'm thinking what do I do . . . do I take an easy paper or do I you know what I mean . . . it's hard. (6/11)

This comment and Harry's subsequent explanation indicated that he considered selecting one of the other subjects he was studying – medieval poetry, religious studies and English literature – to be an 'easier' option than continuing to study Spanish.

## Affect

The second major theme running through Harry's contributions to the interviews is that of his fluctuating affective responses to the course. The role of affect in language learning is well documented (Arnold 1999) and generally understood to play a major role in learning. Initially, Harry was extremely positive about the idea of learning Spanish and of acquiring proficiency in another language. As indicated above, he was particularly enthusiastic about the staff leading the lecture and oral tutorial sessions. However, he was less keen on the audio-visual classes:

> You listen and you repeat and that's it you know. (1/22.00)

He contrasted this apparently tedious experience with the stimulating 'performance' given by the principal lecturer in the lecture sessions. However, Harry admitted to being reluctant to respond to the lecturer's questions, explaining that there were people in the class who were better than he was. This response suggests that he was unwilling to risk making a mistake in the public situation of the class, despite his comment below that he felt little empathy with the majority of his classmates.

Harry's involvement with the Spanish Club was evidence of his overwhelmingly positive attitude to things Spanish. When asked if his club activities might distract him from his study, Harry assured the researcher that, on the contrary, his involvement with the club complemented his study of the language:

> It's kind of throwing yourself into this really cool place . . . and being able to identify a few things with the words you know. (2/13.00)

However, the social context of the course did not appear to contribute positively to Harry's experience. In the very first interview, Harry explained that he felt little rapport with many of his classmates (1/20.00):

> You look around in the lecture theatres and a lot of the people are . . . eighteen to twenty and . . . you know I really don't give a stuff, you know I'll probably never see them again.

This theme surfaced again during the third interview, when Harry explained that collaborating with some of his colleagues in the Spanish Club to organize events was 'like being a kindergarten teacher' (3/18.00). He elaborated by explaining that, of the large number of classmates who had volunteered to be members of the Spanish Club committee, very few had shown any inclination or ability to help with organizing events and performing other functions usually associated with committee membership. During the same interview – almost halfway through the course – Harry explained that whereas he had a classmate in his Religious Studies class with whom he regularly exchanged ideas on the course:

> There's nothing . . . with the Spanish . . . you need someone not only that you can talk to but . . . someone that you actually like I think . . . you need to have some sort of connection there . . . (3/25.00)

110

It was at this point (in the seventh week of the course) that I offered to introduce Harry to a student who was a native speaker of Spanish so that the two could meet for conversation practice. Harry leapt at the opportunity. Throughout the remaining sessions, he remained very positive about his conversation partner, suggesting that he saw their conversations as a way of meeting his social needs, as well as enriching his linguistic environment. Harry never reported making a friend in the Spanish class with whom to study or discuss the course. Given his gregarious nature, this was quite surprising, but could perhaps be explained by the fact that he was several years older than most of the course members and conspicuously more extroverted.

Harry's initially positive attitude towards the Spanish classes began to wane halfway through the trimester, when he reported that the course had stopped being fun and seemed to focus too much on grammar. He claimed not to have spent much time learning verb forms and memorizing vocabulary in the first few weeks of the course and reported that he now realized that this was beginning to pose a problem. In the fifth interview, Harry complained:

> It's just rules . . . that's all it is at this stage, it's not . . . a whole lot of concepts that you've got to sort of unwind and unravel . . . there are no great mysteries . . . the mystery is – how the hell do I remember it all? (5/12.00)

This comment was very revealing of Harry's expectations of the nature of the language learning experience. He appeared to be disappointed with the lack of *conceptual* input which had characterized the early weeks of the course, explaining:

> I don't want . . . completely immerse myself in the grammar, just find it boring, that's horrible but . . . initially it was wonderful, there were all these sounds which er you know and making all these words and there's all these connotations and . . . you just kind of think wow this is really cool and then that kind of novelty . . . it hasn't worn off but . . . you know, the reality of a whole lot of exercises. (4/12.00)

Harry's reaction can be better understood by examining the way in which he had conceptualized language learning at the start of the course (discussed in the next section), and observing how this contrasted with the language learning reality which the course delivered.

## Conceptualization of language learning

At the beginning of the second interview, Harry contrasted his experience of learning French[2] with his study of Spanish. He mentioned, for example, his conviction that the pronunciation of Spanish was easier to 'grasp' than that of French (2/4.00), that French was a lot more 'formal' (2/6.00), that the French course was moving 'very quickly . . . of the two it seems to be the faster' (2/3.00) and (in discussing problems associated with learning the correct gender of nouns) that:

> there's a lot more clues in Spanish . . . than there are in French . . .
> I guess the difference is the rules in Spanish are easier to
> understand or work out for yourself . . . there's a lot more things
> that you've just got to know in French. (2/7.00)

This discussion occurred in the context of Harry explaining why he had decided to withdraw from the French course.

In the third interview – about halfway through the course – a new theme emerged in Harry's characterization of what learning Spanish required. He explained this in terms of 'discipline', saying that 'the Spanish side of the . . . whole study I see er as a disciplinarian thing . . . it's really a er discipline' (3/6.00). He then elaborated:

> you can't just . . . sit there and let your mind . . . spin off onto
> tangents . . . and then write about that. You've got to do it in such
> a way that you can be understood. (3/7.00)

Harry seemed to be referring both to the mental discipline involved in, for example, learning verb paradigms and the gender of nouns in a new language, and to the place that Spanish occupied in his study experience as a whole. Spanish was definitely the 'odd one out' of the courses in which Harry was enrolled, in terms of the type of mental activity it required and the focus of learning. Whereas his other courses encouraged open-ended discussion and speculation, his Spanish course required him to internalize accurately a specified body of knowledge.

Later in the same interview Harry reported having realized that before it is possible to express ideas in a new language it is necessary first to master the language system, which, according to him (3/12.00), is 'the hard part'. He then commented that he hadn't started trying to make jokes in Spanish or to use the language to express his own meanings:

> I probably shouldn't cos it's sort of . . . starts verging on the
> undisciplined approach. (3/16.00)

This intriguing comment seems to suggest that Harry believed it 'undisciplined' to use the new language to express his own ideas. Using the target language to say what he wanted (fluency-focused language use) seemed somehow less legitimate than the accuracy-focused activities apparently favoured in the course. Yet, in the first interview, when asked about the relative importance to him of the goals of fluency and accuracy, Harry had responded, 'the accuracy is important but fluency is crucial' (1/30.00). By the sixth week of the course, the course goals appeared to have replaced his own.

With the benefit of hindsight, in Week 10 of the course, Harry identified one of the elements required for successful language learning as being 'hard work', especially in the first four weeks of the course:

> that's the crucial part of the paper, you've got to hit that hard, if you're going to hit that paper hard at all, you've got to do it then, because if you don't do it then, you're playing catch-up all the way through. (5/19.00)

While he stopped short of admitting that he had spent less time than he had needed to on his Spanish in those early weeks of his course, Harry went on to identify the kind of learning which he believed was required for Spanish. According to him, because of the

> categorical nature of . . . learning something like Spanish . . . you have to learn something small and file it, learn another small and file it . . . In Spanish you can't sit down two nights before and go oh man I've got to learn the whole first er present tense and and the past tense and you know all the words for shopping all the words for food . . . just doesn't work like that. (5/24.00)

The implication is that this systematic, quantitative approach to learning did not suit Harry. The kind of learning, which Harry believed, was necessary for language learning contrasted starkly with his experience studying English literature, where he claimed that 'cramming' sessions could be successful in the short term. In one interview Harry claimed that he could read a book or a poem the night before a tutorial and contribute confidently to a discussion of that work the following day. His excellent English literature grades suggest that he was very successful at studying literature. Clearly, in his view, learning a foreign language demanded a different learning approach involving systematic, cumulative effort over time.

When, during the third interview, Harry commented that it was 'rather sad' that he didn't have a Spanish conversation partner since 'that's really the vehicle that is going to get you places I think with any language' (3/8.00), he was expressing his understanding of the need for language knowledge to be complemented by opportunities for language use. A little later, he added 'it's the conversational thing that . . . I'm finding is . . . starving me at the moment' (3/24.00). In voicing this need, Harry appeared to be seeking not only an opportunity to practise his language skills, but also an outlet for his own ideas. He compared his experience of learning Spanish with the experience of studying his other subjects in the following way:

> I suppose it [Spanish]'s a reversal of these other papers . . . rather
> than . . . chew through your own ideas . . . see if you can chew
> through somebody else's in a very basic sense. (3/11.00)

Two things are striking about this analogy. Firstly, Harry characterized
language learning as essentially a matter of focusing on ideas contributed
by others ('somebody else'). This apparent lack of ownership and of personal relevance could well have affected his motivation. Secondly, Harry
chose the phrase 'in a very basic sense' to describe the approach to ideas
which might occur in the language class. The impoverished intellectual
context of the Spanish course eventually became the overarching theme
of his comments.

In an attempt to explore further Harry's conceptualization of the language learning process as reflected in the course, the researcher asked
him to explain the difference between the various subjects he was studying. In Week 8 of the course, Harry put it like this:

> the English and . . . the Religion, it's real brain food . . . I can
> really sink my teeth into it and I can just sit there and my mind can
> just whizz around at a million miles an hour in a hundred different
> directions at once . . . and all these possible . . . it's just such a . . .
> vast scope . . . it's exciting. (4/24.00)

In stark contrast, Harry reported his experience of the Spanish classes as
follows:

> but now it's it's the routine exercises, exercises, exercises,
> homework, homework, homework . . . it's the discipline side . . .
> so this monotonous sort of drill has . . . been implemented.
> (4/26.00)

The critical difference between Harry's descriptions of the Spanish
course and of his English literature and religious studies classes was that,
in his view, the latter allowed him (perhaps even *required* him) to contribute and integrate his own personal experience and knowledge in
open-ended discussions. The very words he chose to describe his Spanish
classes reflect mechanical, repetitive, uncreative processes. The metaphor
of the machine drilling away monotonously says it all! He described his
English and religious studies papers, on the other hand, in terms of
depth, scope, speed and excitement.

In summarizing what he needed in order to remain motivated when
learning, Harry claimed the 'interest factor' was essential for him, and
the ability actually to use the language. In stark contrast to this idealized
conceptualization, is his view of what was required in order to pass the
Spanish course:

> it's just a matter of doing it, you do it, you learn it, you write it
> down, it's that easy . . . you don't have to learn any grasping

> concepts . . . it's just a matter of remembering a whole lot of stuff I
> suppose. (4/Tape 2/2.00)

While this view of the Spanish course might be termed 'mechanistic',
Harry certainly did not find the course easy. Much of his discourse
reflected the challenge it posed for him. In the fifth interview, when asked
to characterize the challenge which learning Spanish represented for him,
Harry explained:

> it's intellectually demanding in the sense that you've got to
> memorize and contextualize everything that you learn independent
> from the last or the next . . . English has a certain context . . . it
> doesn't change . . . Religion is the same depending on what topic
> you you're looking at . . . and while Spanish is is presented in you
> know shopping one week clothes the next week eating the next
> week . . . it is a different sort of context because you've got to . . .
> you're constantly having to switch your mind from okay verbs in
> the present verbs in the past and then it's like okay well hang on
> there's this mountain of nouns that I'm also supposed to know and
> you know I suppose it does kind of help to have these . . . titles of
> shopping or clothes or food . . . (5/10.00)

What Harry appeared to be reflecting on here was the challenge of
making sense of the course designer's way of organizing and sequencing
material in the course. Clearly the 'hooks' on which course members
were encouraged to hang the lexical and grammatical items presented in
the Spanish classes were not meaningful for him. While he accepted the
course designer's view of what the learning content ought to be, clearly
Harry found it difficult to find coherence in the menu of language items
presented.

In the final session, Harry again contrasted what went on in the
religious studies classes with what happened in his Spanish course,
saying:

> in many ways [the religious studies lecturers are] forcing you to
> look at things that you believe in you know and hold true and . . .
> see them from somebody else's point of view . . . Spanish doesn't
> you know, it's not, it's just not required. (6/24.00)

For *me*, this is one of the most poignant statements of Harry's frustration.
When he signed on for his introductory Spanish course, he expected to be
exploring another world-view. He was hoping to gain some insight into
the literature, art, history and cultural experience of another people.
Instead, he encountered the challenge of attempting to master the language system which, in the end, overshadowed any enjoyment he gained.
While there is no doubt that certain aspects of the course involved appreciation of Hispanic culture, it is equally clear that for Harry the Spanish
course lacked the intellectual challenge of the other courses he was taking.

The last insight into Harry's perspective on the Spanish course arose during the fifth interview, when he proposed an analogy between cooking (in which he was professionally trained and qualified) and language learning. In this extended analogy, Harry identified *memory* and *practice* as attributes of successful cooks and commented that he had no difficulty memorizing recipes. In attempting to explain why he found it hard to memorize vocabulary and grammatical rules, he explained that, when learning to cook, material is first learned theoretically in class, and subsequently put into practice in the environment of a working kitchen. Attempting to remember something abstract can be hard, he explained, but once the knowledge had been applied a number of times in producing a dish, a sauce or a dessert, it became difficult to forget. He later reiterated that when he was learning to cook 'there was definitely the division between working and studying' (5/Side B/17.00). The parallel between the roles of abstract knowledge and practice first in cooking, and then in language learning, is striking. Though he did not spell it out himself, Harry appeared to be saying that successful language learning depends on a balance between the two. It is interesting to speculate about the difference it would have made to Harry's experience of learning Spanish if the course had included more opportunities for learners to use what they knew of the language.

Harry's experience highlights just how problematic beginner-level language learning at university can be. While 'hobby' language classes in which adult learners often enrol carry with them no expectation of intellectual stimulus beyond the satisfaction of being able to use the language for (albeit modest) communication purposes, the same cannot be said of language classes offered at universities. For learners whose goals are to gain a basic proficiency in the language, a university language course such as the one Harry enrolled in may be quite satisfactory. But for those who wish to dream and think and engage with the language, its history and ideas, the experience *may* be a frustrating one.

## Conclusion

As long ago as 1977, Schumann and Schumann (1977) wrote about the potential for the learner's personal agenda in language learning to contrast with that of the teacher. Schumann and Schumann were reporting on their experiences of learning Arabic in Tunisia, and Farsi at UCLA and then in Iran. So, what does studying transcripts of Harry's interviews tell us about his agenda? Firstly, Harry's 'agenda' in enrolling in the introductory Spanish course was part of a broader educational plan for his life. His interest in the language was motivated by a desire to learn about the culture, history and ideas of the Hispanic world, and to explore the linguistic relationship between Spanish and English. Accordingly, the goals that Harry specified in early interviews related broadly to acquiring the ability to use the language to express himself and to explore the culture of the people who spoke the language. Yet the interviews provide evidence of a consistent narrowing of Harry's goals until the course agenda dominated completely, forcing him to reduce his focus to the memorization of grammatical rules. In the fifth interview, Harry revealed that he believed he had a poor memory for grammatical rules, terminology and vocabulary, but not for ideas. Given his belief that much of what is required for successful language learning depends on memory of discrete linguistic items, it is no surprise that, at the end of the course, he was unsure whether he would pass (5/9/.00).

Harry eventually completed the Spanish course with a bare passing grade of 'C'. Yet, in his second and third years at university, he went on to major in English literature, achieving nine 'A' passes, seven 'B' passes, and two 'C' passes (of which Spanish was one) in his subsequent papers. My observations suggest that Harry was a highly original, intelligent, confident, autonomous individual. But the experience of enrolling in this language course was one of narrowing his goals to memorization for survival. The data illustrate that the course carried with it a powerful set of assumptions about the respective roles of teachers and learners, which indicated that goal setting was not the domain of learners.

It seems appropriate to let Harry have the last word. After reading a draft of this chapter, he sent a long e-mail message to the author commenting on various aspects of his experience of learning Spanish at university. Most central to the focus of this chapter was the following remark:

> I personally think that living languages require learners who actively participate in breathing life into them. For me, Spanish was transformed from an enticingly colourful exciting promise into something flat, boring, uninspired and tedious . . . as the course went on, I felt little affinity with my classmates and therefore felt no desire to contribute to their experience . . .

What Harry describes as a 'transformation' was the process by which his personal learning agenda gradually gave way to the course agenda. However, somewhat surprisingly, his 12 weeks of introductory Spanish did not put an end to his interest in the language. Harry concluded his message by reporting: 'I will pursue Spanish, indeed, my girlfriend and I have just enrolled in conversational classes at the community centre around the corner.'

An optimistic conclusion to this study would be to see Harry's agenda as ultimately having survived the university language course he enrolled in. This case study of his language learning experience has highlighted the importance of personal investment in learning. Indeed, the relationship between the learner and the learning experience is particularly crucial in the case of language learning. Norton claims (2000, p. 142):

> It is only by understanding the histories and lived experiences of language learners that the language teacher can create conditions that will facilitate social interaction both in the classroom and in the wider community, and help learners claim the right to speak. Likewise, unless learners believe that their investments in the target language are an integral and important part of the language curriculum, they may resist the teacher's pedagogy, or possibly even remove themselves from the class entirely.

Norton's words are relevant for all language learners. Whether learning a foreign language in their own country, or trying to acquire the majority language of the country in which they are living, learners' contribution to the curriculum – in terms of goals, interest and effort – must be not only acknowledged but also utilized in order for the classroom experience to be meaningful.

## Notes

1. This is the pseudonym which the research subject chose for himself.
2. Harry withdrew from the French course at the end of the second week of the trimester.

# 9 Accommodation zone: Two learners' struggles to cope with a distance learning English course

*Solasa Sataporn and Martin Lamb*

For many working adults around the world, enrolling on a distance course seems a sensible form of academic or professional self-advancement. But isolated from instructor and peers, reliant on packaged materials sent from afar, and with already busy lives to lead, distance learners face severe challenges in making progress in their chosen subject. Language learning by distance can bring particular frustrations of its own, as contemporary methodology puts a high value on communicative language practice with peers, which may be denied to those learning independently. It is perhaps not surprising then that 'distance education is associated in most people's minds with much higher withdrawal rates than are found in conventional face-to-face education' (Woodley, de Lange and Tanewski 2001, p. 113).

Concern with student drop-out was the catalyst for much early research interest in distance education (e.g., Sweet 1986; Bernard and Amundsen 1989), culminating in Kember's model of student progress designed to explain success and failure among adult learners studying at a distance (Kember 1995). This model proposed that a learner's characteristics on entering a course of study – such as their previous educational experience and work conditions – predisposed them either to integrate socially and academically, leading to success, or to attribute their difficulties to features of the course rather than to personal factors, leading ultimately to rejection and drop-out. However, doubts have recently been cast on the ability of this model to explain student progress in a range of different distance education contexts. When Kember's research method was replicated with adult students on a business course at the UK's Open University, for example, the model proved statistically unreliable (Woodley, de Lange and Tanewski 2001). The authors concluded that student drop-out was 'a complex multivariate phenomenon and a process that needed to be understood longitudinally . . . Shortcomings seem inevitable if one attempts to understand a longitudinal process by means of a one-off questionnaire' (ibid., p. 129).

Kember (1999, p. 110) has himself acknowledged that important practical questions remain, in particular why 'some students facing a multitude of conflicting demands seem able to cope with both them and their course, while others, apparently under considerably less pressure, fall by the wayside'. Further, he suggests that answering such questions

119

'undoubtedly requires reaching understanding of a complex, multifaceted scenario through an exploratory enquiry . . . using semi-structured interviews with students' (ibid., p. 111). What he found through analysis of learners' own words was that 'students are not pre-destined to remain in one or other category [i.e., bound towards success or failure] because of their background characteristics' but can use various coping mechanisms – such as sacrificing some element of their current lives, or seeking support from family members – to overcome difficult circumstances (ibid., p. 114). Other students 'who appear to have very favourable circumstances fail to accommodate even quite moderate study demands', because they do not employ these coping mechanisms (ibid.).

Kember's (1999) study suggests that qualitative research which relies on analysis of a limited number of first-person accounts may be able to show the true complexity of learning experiences more clearly than large-scale quantitative surveys. In particular, it emphasizes the role of social context, interacting with psychological characteristics, in explaining individual learning behaviour. In the field of independent adult language learning, Norton (2000) conducted a longitudinal case study of immigrant women learning English in Canada and concluded that success or failure depended far less on individual traits such as aptitude or motivation than on their ability to negotiate access to English-speaking social networks, at work or elsewhere. Studies of *distance* foreign language learners are rare, but one recently published work also took a qualitative approach, aiming 'to reveal how the learner experiences, interprets and apprehends self-instructed language learning' through a longitudinal series of interviews, open-ended questionnaires and other techniques eliciting the 'insider's perspective' (White 1999, p. 445). In this way White was able to show how learners' beliefs and expectations about their course are modified by the learning experience – though she also concludes that predispositions, such as tolerance of ambiguity and locus of control, help to determine their ability to adapt to the demands of the course.

We hope to add to this growing body of qualitative research by reporting here an investigation into how 42 adult language learners coped with the demands of their distance course at a higher education institute in Thailand (Sataporn 2000). The rest of this chapter will describe the context and method of the study, present the main findings and provide evidence in the form of two first-person accounts, one from a student who seemed to be making good progress, the other from a student who eventually dropped out. Finally we will discuss the implications of the study for course designers and researchers in the field of distance language learning.

## Research context

The study was carried out by one of the authors at Sukhothai Thammathirat Open University (STOU) in Bangkok, Thailand, where she works as a lecturer in English language. The institute offers a one-year Certificate in English for a Specific Career Programme, with ten job-specific courses offered (e.g., English for Tourism, English for Law). To obtain the certificate, students need to pass five different courses, by working through self-study packages and attending a maximum of three optional tutorial sessions per course in their own regions (though the availability of tutorials depends on sufficient numbers of students). The five courses can be completed in one calendar year, or over a maximum of three years. Despite this flexibility, fewer than 15% of the two thousand or more students who enroll on the programme each year actually complete the course and obtain the certificate. This high drop-out rate provides a strong practical motive for researching the learning experience of students.

## Methods of data collection and analysis

The aim of the study was to describe the learning behaviour of students taking a self-instructional distance English programme at the university and to identify factors which affected this behaviour, including their continued participation. The approach was descriptive and interpretive, in that it sought to understand how individual learners perceived the course and how they themselves explained their behaviour in context and over time.

Data was collected by following one group of informants, comprising 36 students, over six months of their involvement in the one-year programme – some during their first six months, some during their second six months. Semi-structured interviews were conducted with each student, at the beginning and end of the six-month period. In addition, twelve of the informants were persuaded to write 'study diaries', in order to record the regularity and thoroughness of their studying. Finally, the longitudinal data was supplemented by a cross-sectional study of students who had already completed the programme (or were doing resit examinations) and who had one-off interviews with the researcher in which they reflected on their learning behaviour and progress.

As the informants were mostly glad to have the opportunity to discuss their work and progress with a sympathetic but knowledgeable listener, the interviews generated large amounts of data. The study diaries, on the other hand, tended to be rather superficial, though they were useful as a means of cross-checking the information from the interviews. The data were analysed through a rigorous process of coding and re-coding, until categories and themes emerged, allowing eventually for the conceptualization of models which could be applied to almost all the individual cases. The next section summarizes the main findings of the study, which we will then illustrate by reference to individual cases.

## Findings

The learners' accounts of their experience on the course centred around three main themes: the *appropriateness*, the *difficulty* and the *demands* of studying on the distance programme. These were the issues which, in their perception, ultimately determined whether they would persist in studying or drop out. They arose as soon as they started studying, out of the interaction between components of their own personality and lives, and features of the programme. We can present the learner and programme components within a pair of overlapping oval shapes, as in Figure 9.1.

The findings of our study suggest that learners' success in the STOU programme depends greatly on whether they can find an accommodation between the STOU components and the components of their own lives. They do this by adjusting their components and STOU components so that they mesh or merge with each other harmoniously. However, this accommodation is not fixed but *dynamic*, as shown by the bi-directional dotted arrow. The more learners are able to adjust the components of their learner zone and/or those in the STOU zone to mesh with one another, the better they can construct an accommodation zone – that is, an imaginary space where the learner's personal priorities and the academic requirements of the course are both met. As they move through the programme, learners will constantly be having to make readjustments to preserve or expand this accommodation zone.

The three themes of appropriateness, difficulty and demands are like the discordant noises that emerge when the two shapes fail to mesh harmoniously and instead grate against each other. Thus, learners talk about the *appropriateness* of the course when there is a clash between their personal culture of English language learning – that is, their beliefs, expectations and goals, as well as relevant aspects of their personality – and certain programme components, which might include learning materials, class organization, teaching methodology, syllabus content, course assignments or a range of other pedagogical and practical matters. They talk about the *difficulty* of the course when there is a clash between the personal culture

COMPONENTS INVOLVED IN STUDYING

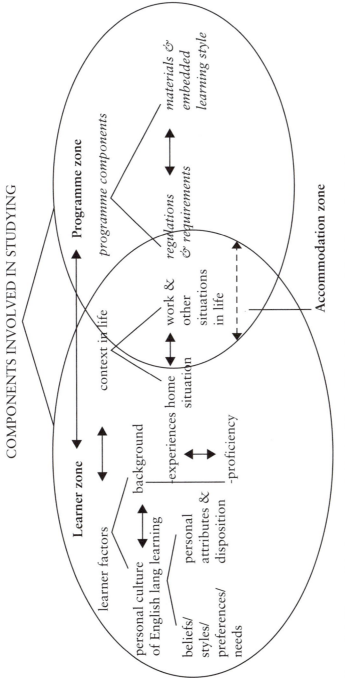

**Figure 9.1** The model of components involved in studying behaviours and their inter-relationship

of learning, their background (especially current proficiency level) and programme components. And they talk about the *demands* of the course when there is a clash between their personal culture of learning, their context in life and programme components.

We will now demonstrate the working of this model by presenting extracts from the first-person accounts of two students on the STOU course. Although two individuals cannot exemplify all the processes that were observed in the larger population, we hope that by creating rounded, contextualized portraits of individuals readers will be able to identify with them and relate the ideas more easily to their own experience or context of work. Both learners were interviewed just before they began the course, and at the end of the first semester, when they had taken the first two courses – Foundation English and Reading in English. Neither of them completed study diaries.

### Case 1: Tanong

Tanong[1] is a single man of 38 who lives alone in his rented flat. He has a bachelor's degree in law from an open university, though that programme was not purely self-instructional. He now works as a lawyer in the government taxation office, and part-time as a consultant in a law firm. At STOU, his major was in English for Law. At the end of the first semester, he finished studying all the materials without skipping any parts. He viewed his proficiency in English as very low but was very confident in his ability to study by himself:

> One day, we will be able to stand proudly and feel smarter than everyone or most people or smarter than the person who graduated in this field or majored in English. That may be true. It depends on effort . . . how hard we try.

He viewed English as a key to better career prospects, since he would then be able to offer legal consultancies to foreigners working or doing business in Thailand. As a single man, he stated, he had no burdens and therefore could afford to pay for academic courses:

> Investing money on education will be an investment that brings results in the future.

At the second interview after the end of the first semester, he expressed his satisfaction with the programme so far in this way:

> We have to help ourselves like this. But in fact I want it . . . really really want it because . . . to tell you again . . . even if I have to pay more I wouldn't mind.

*Case 2: Ladda*

Ladda (24 years old) is also single and lives with her parents. She received her bachelor's degree in banking from a vocational college just before joining the STOU programme. She works as an accountant in a government enterprise office, a career chosen for her by her parents:

> I never thought of working here before and I didn't like accountancy either. But as for English, I like it since I was young. And I like art.

She thought that a Master's degree may enable her to change the direction of her career, though she was not sure exactly where she wanted to go. English is important because the Master's programme may be in English, and there will certainly be an entrance exam in English:

> . . . I also want to continue for a Master's degree.
>
> Q: In which field?
>
> It may not be in (business) administration . . . but as for a Master's in art, it is impossible . . . so I am interested in IT . . . something like that.
>
> Q: If there are programmes in English and in Thai, which will you choose?
>
> Now my foundation in English is not quite . . . not really good.
>
> Q: What do you mean 'your foundation is not good'?
>
> It is as if I've completely disregarded it. But I started studying by myself by buying books from the book centre . . .

She seemed to be determined to improve her English, and enrolling on the STOU programme was an expression of this desire. However, at the second interview, after one semester's work, she explained that she had decided to drop out of the programme.

Thus, these two students both appeared to the researcher at the beginning of the programme to have high motivation to study. Yet after a single semester, one of them was so enthusiastic that he would even accept increased fees, while the other had already quit. We can find an explanation for this surprising outcome by analysing the way they talked about the three main issues and their struggles to create accommodation zones.

*Appropriateness of the programme*

Learners construct their personal cultures of learning partly from their experience in studying. As this was the first true distance programme for both learners, they can be viewed as entering a new culture of learning. Their successful completion of the programme would depend partly on whether they could find an accommodation between these two 'cultures'.

Tanong conceded after the first semester that the programme had been a novel experience:

> I even feel that this is a new style . . . a new style that I had never come across before.

He made no explicit statement that this new style was appropriate to him, but the way he talked about it shows that he was engaged in a struggle to reshape his own personal culture of English language learning in the learner zone so that it meshed with the culture of learning in the programme zone:

> STOU textbooks are rather complete. The contents cover many things . . . except that having no 'class' makes me unsure that what we read and understand is correct according to the principle or not. And the textbooks are close to everyday life such as newspapers . . . job applications . . . advertisements. Using these media brings it close to our life. When we read the *Bangkok Post*, we understand some but not other parts. We will recall that we have seen it in the newspaper and when we compare them, it will make us understand more deeply. When attending 'class' and listening to the lecturer, it will be deeper. Our idea will go up another step. Actually, it's not just English . . . other subjects as well, attending 'class' and listening to the lecturer is necessary. It helps a lot. It is just because this is an 'open university' . . .
>
> Q: Do you learn according to the suggested steps?
>
> Yes. I do everything.
>
> Q: Do you have to rewind the tape when listening?
>
> I rewind it. That is . . . when reading the book, I will do what the tape and the book instruct.

In this typically dense passage Tanong showed appreciation of the programme materials but regretted the lack of classroom contact with a lecturer. Despite this serious clash with his preferred style of learning, he followed the course instructions to the letter.

In contrast, Ladda viewed the programme as irrelevant in terms of learning style, the contents of one of the courses, and the method of teaching:

> Learning by myself . . . it is a foundation as I have told you . . . that is . . . my nature is like . . . I have to be stimulated. If I read by myself at home like this, when picking it (the book) up, sometimes I feel sleepy . . . sometimes bored . . . sometimes I even fall asleep.

Clearly there is a clash between the programme culture and her personal culture of learning. One potential source of conflict is noticeable in her first interview:

> I was impressed by English teachers since I was at kindergarten. Then at Pratom (primary school) I was also impressed . . . at Mattayom (secondary school) I was also impressed . . . I was impressed that the teachers taught well.

Having this very positive attitude towards teachers may have predisposed her against self-instruction as an appropriate mode of study. In the next extract, we see her struggling to adapt her learning style to the programme:

> As for units 6–7, I haven't read them at all. I think that I will wait until the tutor teaches that part and when the tutor emphasizes any points, I will also focus on that and I will come back to read it by myself . . . revise by myself because if I have to read right away . . . it is like doing it without an aim. If I have listened to the tutor emphasising something, when I get back . . . they are the points.

Another component of the course that did not suit her were the audio tapes:

> I like the Reading (course) but this one (Foundation English) has tapes. In some units that require listening to the tape, I don't like them.

Again, struggling to find an accommodation with the course, she avoided doing the listening exercises as far as possible, seeing if she could get by without them.

Furthermore she did not like the way that introductions and explanations in the textbooks are written in the Thai language. She suggested improving the books in this way:

> Maybe . . . reduce . . . reduce the (Thai) language . . . If changing from Thai into English . . . all . . . all . . . all the books . . . I think that if it is in English it will be more interesting because when it is in Thai, we don't want to read that part and then we can't do the exercises.

It seems that the STOU textbooks did not match her expectations about what English language materials should be like, because they include a lot of Thai language. At the second interview, after one semester of study, she found further fault with the materials, which did not match up to those she had used in the past:

> (STOU should) improve the contents of the books . . . for example . . . let me compare . . . for example TUGET at Thammasart

> (University) . . . they will present each (grammatical point) in the topic. If it is 'structure', they present the 'subject' in one topic . . . that is . . . the details are only about the 'subject'.

The STOU textbooks give practice in the four skills and present grammatical points only as adjuncts to this skills-development work. But past experience in the classroom, as well as self-study materials that she had bought in the marketplace, had led to the strong expectation that textbooks will present grammatical structures in a methodical way. Her frustration was increased by the fact that she was going to take an entrance test for a Master's programme which would have a heavy grammar component.

In summary, we have seen here three examples of how Ladda's personal culture of learning clashed with that of the programme – there were no teachers, she was forced to use audio tapes, and the course textbook lacked a core grammatical syllabus. By the end of the first semester, the clash of cultures was so profound that she was unable to create an accommodation zone, and she sought and found a course that seemed more appropriate.

### Difficulty level

Many of the informants in the study revealed problems in relation to the difficulty of the STOU programme. Tanong, for example, claimed that the course was initially too challenging. The first problem he found, after just one week of the course, was vocabulary:

> I get stuck at the vocabulary and when I scan, oh . . . vocabulary . . . oh . . . vocabulary. I can't understand. I can't answer the questions. Success does not occur at this point.

However, he immediately set about devising a solution to this problem:

> So vocabulary . . . I think . . . vocabulary. So I have to memorize vocabulary first and read the book later so that I can understand . . . so that I can get it . . . I have one separate vocabulary notebook. At noon, I sit and memorize the vocabulary . . . I sit and memorize the vocabulary.

His solution was to do extra work, in his own way, to make up for his perceived deficiency. In other words, he was prepared to reduce a component in his learner zone – his relaxation time at the noon break – in order to find an accommodation with components of the programme zone. However, at the second interview he showed how the Reading course itself had also helped him find an accommodation. In dealing with difficult reading texts, he had adopted a new strategy:

> I feel more confident because I know that if I can't understand this one, I can skip reading it and read until finishing (the whole text)

first . . . one time first . . . to find what is in it . . . and then try again . . . and we will get it without any difficulties.

For Ladda, difficulty level was not a major issue. However, she did find that one course was not challenging enough and actually dug out some materials from a previous course to study.

> to tell you the truth . . . normally when reading (Foundation English) . . . I read up to only unit 2 . . . not read much . . . and the content is not concise . . . the book . . . it is like it is not precise . . . so I bring out the old materials which I have collected since Mattayom (secondary school) (to study).

By the time of her second interview, she had given up with STOU materials and had found a new course which presented the right level of challenge:

> this makes me turn to pay attention to Thammasart . . . because they have a test as well.
>
> Q: They also have a test?
>
> Yes.
>
> Q: How do they learn?
>
> They learn and there is a test in between (units).
>
> Q: What do they focus on?
>
> They focus on taking an exam to continue our studies at Thammasart . . . TUGET.
>
> Q: Yes. And they have a test and textbooks?
>
> The test is not often but it is detailed. Sometimes I can't catch up. Sometimes, the vocabulary in the subject . . . like the teacher just skips over (the unknown words) on and on . . . but I don't know so I have to come and read.

## The demands of studying

The third issue which emerged from learners' accounts as pivotal to their successful study was whether they could accommodate the demands of the programme into their often very busy lives as working adults. Again, Tanong and Ladda provide contrasting views of the learning experience.

Although Tanong had one of the most demanding work schedules among the course participants, with both full-time and part-time jobs in the legal profession, he showed from the beginning that he was willing to accept the physical demands of the programme. In fact, he almost seems to have relished the challenge. He believes that being a distance student requires above all great self-discipline:

> It is all right no matter how thick the book is because the students who come to study have to be readers . . . diligent in reading. When we have time, we read and read. When it's time to work, I work. When I read I forget about work. I read very often. When I have time, I read. I read until I am tired and I sleep. I read, read, read, read, read, read no matter whether I understand or not. When I have time, I read. And I repeat it like that. Then I will remember it automatically.

His personal culture of learning was probably influenced by his experience of studying law, where he learned effectively by memorization and repetition. He found that this strategy could be applied to learning English in self-instructional mode, enabling him to work his way methodically through the materials unit by unit. That he quickly reached a satisfactory accommodation with the demands of the programme is evidenced by the fact that, at the end of the first semester, he was still offering to pay more in order to be able to study more:

> I still confirm that if possible . . . I want to pay more money for learning every Saturday and Sunday

In contrast, Ladda did not expect that the programme would be demanding:

> I didn't know before . . . when the books arrived . . . oh . . . shocked . . . four books.
>
> Q: You didn't expect that there would be so many books?
>
> No, I thought there would only be handouts or something like that.

Although her parents were supportive of her study, and even encouraged her to read more, the physical demands of studying created a conflict with her current work context:

> There is . . . this . . . this period . . . I start forgetting already because I don't read much. And now it is the time for balancing the accounts so I am very busy. During these 2–3 weeks, I haven't read the book at all because I am busy and work is busy.
>
> Q: So when you get back home, you feel tired already?
>
> I am tired and I even have to bring work to do at home. It seems like stealing my time because at home . . . it is like . . . if I am at home . . . if I am free, I will read. And when I bring the work to do, I don't read at all.

She considered that her work 'stole' her study time at home. In other words, she had failed to find an accommodation between her context in life and the components of the programme.

## Summary

Tanong was able to create a large accommodation zone in between the learner zone and the programme zone. Like almost all the students, he discusses the relative appropriateness, difficulty level and demands of this academic course, and from his account we can see how he has managed to find a fit between components of his learner zone and those of the programme zone. In this necessarily brief sketch, we have seen how his disposition to be persistent in studying, his professional need for English, his learning strategies developed through previous academic courses and his high level of disposable income all helped him find this accommodation with the programme. There were also aspects of the learner zone which worked against this accommodation – for example, his busy work schedule and his low proficiency level – but these were outweighed by the positive components. As a result, we were very confident that he would complete the course, even if he had to resit some examinations.[2]

Ladda failed to create an accommodation zone. Her original motivation for joining the programme was to gain access to and study on an English-medium Master's degree, and the STOU programme did not seem to be serving this need. Furthermore, her personal culture of language learning predisposed her to favour teacher-led classes, and towards a demanding grammar-based syllabus. At first she did try to find an accommodation with the programme, by skipping those components which didn't suit her learning preferences – the audio tapes and the Thai explanations. She also supplemented the course with her own bought materials. As time went by, however, her frustration led her to seek out an alternative course. When she found a suitable one, she decided to give up trying to accommodate to the STOU programme and enrolled in this new programme.

Interestingly, she did not make an external attribution for her dropping out, as Kember's model (1995) would predict. Instead she blamed herself, concluding her second interview with these sad words:

> I feel sorry that I can't do this. Why can't we do it? . . . something like that. At first I thought that I would be able to manage but, when trying, it is not like that.

## Implications of the study

In this final section of this paper, we briefly consider the implications of this study for course designers and for future researchers in the field. Firstly, it is noteworthy that this qualitative study of distance language learning has identified the same three key issues in learners' experiences

131

of distance learning as a recent quantitative study. Drawing conclusions from her own evaluation of resource-based learning, Thorpe (1996, p. 136) argues:

> It is important for those creating materials and making changes to them to understand not only the percentage of responses on particular issues such as *difficulty, workload, relevance or interest,* but what is behind the response and what drives the diversity between learners of the same materials [our italics].

*Difficulty, workload* and *relevance* clearly correspond with the themes that emerged in this study, namely difficulty, demands and appropriateness.

First-hand accounts by learners, such as those reported here, reveal the extent of this 'diversity between learners'. Indeed, they show how discord and unease may be a natural part of the first stages of a distance programme (or any other 'novel' type of educational experience) as learners struggle to create an accommodation zone. Based on this data, course designers at STOU are now working out ways to increase the potential for accommodation. More detailed orientation materials before students begin the course, more optional elements within the course design, and the opportunity for one-to-one counselling for students who are thinking of dropping out – such innovations could help students come to perceive the course as more appropriate, at the right difficulty level, and not too demanding on their time.

In-depth explorations of individuals' experiences also uncover the complexity of the relationships between factors linked to success and failure. For example, it is often assumed that 'some degree of autonomy is a prerequisite for success in self-instruction' (Benson 2001, p. 132). Yet we see here two learners who are autonomous in different ways. Tanong is self-reliant, is prepared to make sacrifices in his private life to accommodate the course and has firm views about how he learns best. At the same time he appears to follow the course instructions slavishly. Ladda appears to be more aware of her own needs as a learner, adopts a more critical view of the materials and uses them in a more independent way. It is true that she prefers to have a teacher to motivate and guide her learning. But she is aware of this, and it could be said that she expresses her autonomy most dramatically by dropping out of the programme in order to sign up for a more suitable course. First-hand accounts such as these demonstrate the dangers of making easy associations between single learner characteristics and success, for in these two portraits we see autonomy associated with both 'success' and 'failure'. The effect of such characteristics will always be mediated by a range of other components in the learner and programme zones.

Finally, the two learners presented here also illustrate some dangers inherent in this kind of study, which is dependent upon the lengthy elicitation of learners' experiences in their own words. As Block (2000, p. 760) has pointed out, learners may use such interviews for their own purposes, depending on how they see the interviewer. Tanong, for example, used the interviews to push for changes to the course structure to include more weekend sessions, while Ladda used the interviews to express her complaints, even anger, about course content. Tanong quickly established a rapport with the interviewer, which led to him talking at great length; by contrast, Ladda never relaxed and restricted her comments to short responses to the interviewer's prompts. Furthermore, taking part in the interviews may have helped to shape their subsequent behaviour. Tanong may have been prompted by the questioning about his study habits to become more aware of his own preferences, in turn affecting future behaviour on the course; the interviewer's probing of Ladda's early misgivings about the course may have actually contributed to the build-up of frustration which eventually caused her to drop out.

## Conclusion

Despite these limitations, we hope in this paper to have presented faithfully the self-reported experiences of two distance language students in Thailand. Tanong and Ladda have been used to exemplify or 'personify' the experience of many other students, as they struggle to come to terms with the demands of the distance programme. The struggle seemed to centre on three main areas: the appropriateness of the course, the difficulty level and the practical demands of studying. This struggle, we have suggested, can be seen as an attempt by learners to build an accommodation zone between components of their own lives and those of the programme. The way these components interact determine their success on the programme. However, the sharper our focus on individuals, the more complex these interactions appear. For those delivering such programmes, this conclusion offers no easy solutions to the problem of frequent drop-out; rather it confirms that there will be no easy solution.

## Notes

1. The names of both cases have been changed.
2. We have subsequently heard that Tanong did keep studying until the end of the course, and then for a one-year extension – but still failed to pass all his exams. He was therefore unable to obtain his certificate. It seems that the mandatory four-year time limit was the one component of the STOU programme zone which he could not accommodate to.

# 10 Learning a second language with broadcast materials at home: Japanese students' long-term experiences

*Tae Umino*

This paper explores the experiences of 20 Japanese learners attempting to learn a second language (L2) through self-instruction using broadcast materials. L2 self-instruction using television and radio language courses is widespread, particularly in foreign language learning contexts where access to target language input is limited. In Japan, a considerable number of such materials in various formats are produced each year and learners of an L2 very frequently seek to study by such means (see, for example, Ohkushi 1991; Hara 1992; Umino 1999; and NHK 2002 on the popularity of these types of materials).

Despite this popularity, there have been very few studies which explore what learners actually do when they are learning with such materials. Self-instruction has received little serious attention in general from researchers in L2 teaching (Jones 1998). Jones (1998) also points to the difficulty of getting hold of 'real home-learners' for research purposes. The majority of studies to date have tended to be large-scale close-ended surveys conducted in collaboration with broadcasting companies – see, for example, Rybak (1983), Hill (1976, 1978a, 1978b), Hill and Truscott (1979), Flavell and Fearn (1995), Flavell and Micallef (1995), Lyle and Ogawa (1990) and Ohkushi (1991). Thus, what goes on in the actual learning setting of self-instruction is largely unknown. This chapter attempts to uncover the manner in which learners pursue self-instruction at home by using exploratory in-depth interviews with a view to shedding light on how L2 learning is maintained or abandoned in non-institutional settings.

## Persistence in self-instruction

In this chapter, self-instruction is defined as a mode of instructed learning in which individuals take the initiative for learning without the direction of an educational institution. It is a mode of instructed learning (and *not* natural acquisition) since it involves a 'planned attempt to intervene in the learning process' (Ellis 1990, p. 40) but one that takes place outside of institutionalized educational systems. Thus it differs from *distance learning* in which learners are directed by an institution from a distance even though there is no teacher present in the learning setting. (See Umino 2002, for more discussion on different modes of instructed learning.)

In this non-institutional learning mode, learners appear to face difficulty in persisting in learning itself. Kanfer and Ackerman (1989) describe *persistence* as an aspect of motivation and define it as the extent to which attentional effort is maintained over time, in contrast to *intensity*, which concerns the degree to which effort is directed to the task. And persistence is identified as one of the major challenges for self-instructing learners in studies dealing with 'dropout' in the use of self-instructional courses. Rybak (1980, 1983) summarizes a series of studies carried out to evaluate BBC television and radio language courses in the UK by researchers at Brighton Polytechnic (Hill 1976, 1978a, 1978b; Hill and Truscott 1979) and the University of York (Hawkins, Howson and Green 1976, 1977, 1978). She indicates that the estimated dropout[1] rates for the series evaluated were high (ranging from 25% to 60%) and identifies learner isolation as the major cause of withdrawal. Booker and Bur's (1982) survey also gave a pessimistic estimate that only half of their 1003 respondents had followed all or most of the series investigated. Jones (1996, 1998), based on a factor analysis of a survey administered to 70 adult learners in the UK, argued that the learners often combined self-instruction and classroom learning and that dropout correlated highly with self-instruction alone.

Similar problems have been identified in the use of NHK (Japan Broadcasting Corporation) language courses in the Japanese context. For example, Ohkushi (1991), Ohkushi and Hara (1991) and Hara (1992) report that 36.7% of the 3085 respondents to their survey reported using educational broadcast materials in the five preceding years, but that 30% of these users reported having the experience of dropping out. In my own study with 138 Japanese university students (Umino 1999), 38% of instances of beginning to follow a course were reported to have been abandoned before completion.

While the problem of dropout requires serious consideration, the question of how persistence is made possible under the same circumstances remains unanswered. In my questionnaire-based study, 62% of the reported cases involved course completion and the majority (66%) of the users of broadcast materials reported having completed more than two courses on more than one language (Umino 1999). In cases of such use of multiple series, the learners are assumed to have, at least in part, followed one series after the other continuously over an extended period of time. In addition, the problem of 'isolation' was not indicated in students' responses to a question asking what problems they found with this mode of learning.

Advantages
- Learning is kept regular (by having a fixed time and pace of broadcasts).
- Learning is cheap.
- You can learn at home.
- You can record the programmes.
- Lessons are frequent.
- It is easy to access.

Problems
- It is not interactive.
- You have no control over time of learning.
- You have no control over pace of learning/speed of progress.
- There is no pressure to study.
- You cannot catch up if you miss a lesson.
- You tend to get passive.

**Figure 10.1** Major advantages and problems in the use of broadcast materials

Furthermore, in the survey, I found an interesting paradox that the reasons used by some learners to explain dropout were also used by others to explain persistence (Figure 10.1). For example, the problem of the time of the broadcast being fixed mentioned by some students was reported by others as an advantage which enabled them to follow the series in a regular manner. Similarly, the pace of the lessons being decided for them by an external teacher was seen as lack of control over pace by some, but was perceived to be advantageous by others. The reason for these paradoxes remained unclear. In arriving at a better understanding of the problem of dropout and finding ways of coping with this problem, it seemed necessary to understand how persistence is made possible by solving paradoxes such as these.

## The study

### Aim of the study

The aim of the study was to gain insights into factors which play a role in persistence in self-instruction by investigating the manners in which both the successful and unsuccessful persisters carried out the task of studying with broadcast materials. As I did not have a set hypothesis, I decided to obtain a precise description of learners' past learning experiences of using broadcast materials, narrated by the learners themselves, in the hope of uncovering factors which might be important. I decided to use interviews since their flexibility was considered to be advantageous for the aim described above (discussed further below). By employing this exploratory approach, I hoped to gain new insights which had not been uncovered in the structured surveys which have dominated investigations in this field.

## Participants

The participants in the study were selected from among the 138 respondents in my earlier questionnaire study (Umino 1999) based on their experiences. The following factors were considered in order to obtain a group of students with a variety of experiences:

- course completion / withdrawal from a course
- use of radio only / use of television only / use of both radio and television
- use of a number of series / use of a few series
- studying just one language / studying more than one language using broadcast materials

Having considered the above, 20 participants were selected from among those who had indicated willingness to be interviewed in response to a questionnaire item. All the students were language majors and generally shared a high interest in languages. Their experiences, particularly those of the successful persisters, may not represent those of typical Japanese university students, but since the study hoped to investigate the cases of 'good persisters' (in parallel to 'good language learners'), this was regarded as appropriate.

## The interview

In the interview, participants were asked to describe in detail their learning experiences for each of the television/radio series they mentioned having used in the questionnaire. The interviews were carried out in a semi-structured fashion, that is, basic topics were set to be covered, but elaboration or introduction of new topics by the interviewee was allowed for. The topics set were (1) when, (2) where, (3) for how long, (4) how regularly and (5) why participants had studied using the particular series, (6) what they did as they listened to / watched the programmes, (7) what efforts they made in order to continue their study and (8) their general feelings about the series. The interviews were conducted in Japanese (the participants' mother tongue), recorded onto audio tape, and transcribed for analysis. The extracts presented in this chapter were translated into English by me. The participants are represented by pseudonyms.

## Students' histories of learning with broadcast materials

In analysing the data, I first constructed a full record of each participant's learning history with regard to each of the series they reported having used. From this, four patterns emerged in the ways participants pursued their study, and the participants were grouped into the following groups according to these patterns: 'Early starter / Late completers'; 'Early starters / Late non-completers'; 'Late starters'; and 'Non-completers'. Figure 10.2 shows the learning histories of eight students (two from each group) to illustrate these four patterns, showing the period during which broadcast series were followed continuously, indicated by the years in the school system, with E5 corresponding to age 10, E6, age 11 and so on.[2]

The Early starters / Late completers started using broadcast materials at an early age, between 10 to 13 (that is, fifth year of primary school to first year of junior high school), and had continued using one series or another regularly up to the time of the interview. These students had used broadcast materials in their L2 learning continuously over 6 to 10 years, about one third to half of their lifetime (all the students were between 19 and 23 years old). For example, Aiko started using an English series at sixth grade (age 12) and continued following one series or another until the second year of university (age 20). Six students belonged to this group.

The Early starters / Late non-completers started using broadcast materials before entering high school, and had continued using the series for a fairly long period of two to four years. But they had not continued using them after entering university in as regular and continuous a manner as the Late completers. Kayo, for example, used English series from age 12 to 15 and attempted to start again during university with English, Russian and French, but she did not manage to complete any of them. Five students belonged to this group.

The Late starters began using the series at a later age, after entering high school, and continued using all or most of them regularly for a relatively shorter period of one to three years, thus extending into their university years. Mitsuyo, for example, studied English, French and Italian for one year each during university. Four students belonged to this group.

Finally, the Non-completers were those who had never managed to complete a single series regularly regardless of their age. Masuo, for example, attempted to study with English and Russian series but withdrew in both cases. Five students belonged to this group.

The learning histories of the four groups described above provided useful points of reference for subsequent analysis. The first point was the age factor. In order to see whether there was any substantial difference depending on the age at which students engaged in learning with broad-

Grade (E = Elementary  JH = Junior High  HS = High school  U = University)
●——● Courses completed  ●——→ Courses not completed

**Early starters/Late completers**

| Name | Language | E5 | E6 | JH1 | JH2 | JH3 | HS1 | HS2 | HS3 | U1 | U2 | U3 | U4 |
|---|---|---|---|---|---|---|---|---|---|---|---|---|---|
| Miwako | English | | | | ●——|——|——|——|——|——|—● | | |
| | German | | | | | ●—|—● | | ●—|—|—● | | |
| | Chinese | | | | | | | | ●—|—● | | |
| | Russian | | | | | | | | ●—● | | | |
| Aiko | English | | ●—|——|——|——|——|——|——|——|—● | | |
| | Chinese | | | | | | | | ●—● | | | |

**Early starters/Late non-completers**

| Name | Language | E5 | E6 | JH1 | JH2 | JH3 | HS1 | HS2 | HS3 | U1 | U2 | U3 | U4 |
|---|---|---|---|---|---|---|---|---|---|---|---|---|---|
| Kayo | English | | ●—|——|——|——|—● | | ●↔ | | | |
| | Russian | | | | | | | | | | | ●↔ | |
| | French | | | | | | | | ●↔ | | | |
| Rika | English | | ●—|——|——|—● | | | | | | |
| | French | | | | | | | | | | | ●↔ | |

**Late starters/Late completers**

| Name | Language | E5 | E6 | JH1 | JH2 | JH3 | HS1 | HS2 | HS3 | U1 | U2 | U3 | U4 |
|---|---|---|---|---|---|---|---|---|---|---|---|---|---|
| Koichi | English | | | | | | ●—|—● | | | | |
| | French | | | | | | | ●—|—|—● | | | |
| | German | | | | | | | ●—|—|—● | | | |
| | Chinese | | | | | | | | | ●—|—● | |
| Mitsuyo | English | | | | | | | | | ●—|—● | |
| | French | | | | | | | | | ●—|—● | |
| | Italian | | | | | | | | | ●—|—● | |

**Non-completers**

| Name | Language | E5 | E6 | JH1 | JH2 | JH3 | HS1 | HS2 | HS3 | U1 | U2 | U3 | U4 |
|---|---|---|---|---|---|---|---|---|---|---|---|---|---|
| Junko | English | | ●↔ | | | | | ●↔ | | | |
| | French | | | | | | | | | | | ●↔ | |
| Masuo | English | | | | ●↔ | | | | | | |
| | Russian | | | | | | | | ●↔ | | | |

**Figure 10.2** Students' L2 learning histories using broadcast materials

cast materials, their experiences in their early years was contrasted to those in their later years. The second point was previous experience. In looking at students' experiences in university years, for example, the experiences of the Early starters, who already had long experience of learning with broadcast materials, were contrasted to those of the Late starters, who had only recently begun, to see whether this resulted in any differences. And finally, the experiences of the Non-completers were contrasted to those of students in the other three groups (or the 'Persisters') to cater for factors relating to success or failure in persistence.

I present my analysis below by dividing learners' accounts according to learning with broadcast materials prior to university and during university years as substantial differences were observed between these two time periods in terms of learning management.

## Learning with broadcast materials prior to university

The students who were engaged in using broadcast materials before entering university consisted of the eleven Early starters (six Late completers and five Late non-completers) and four Non-completers. The descriptions of the learning environment by the Early starters have some features in common which seem significant for understanding the issue of persistence.

### *Regularity of time and place of learning*

First, as we observe in extract (1), the Early starters usually listened to or watched the series at a fixed time of day, at the time of the broadcast (see also Figure 10.3).

> (1) Every day, I came back home about six o'clock [pm] and I went and sat at the dining table. My mother was cooking dinner and the radio was on. And at ten past six, the series started with that music and I was there so I naturally listened to it. My mother was also there and we would repeat after the models together. Later, my younger sister joined us and we three would hang around there and listen and repeat together. (Miwako)

In addition, the students also had a fixed place within their homes for listening to or watching the series. Interestingly, students said that, although they had their own bedroom, they tended to listen or watch in the kitchen area[3] or living rooms, where there were other family members around, as we observed in extract (1). In an extreme case, one student, Chiaki, reported that the whole family collaborated together to keep listening to a radio series:

> (2) It [the series] was on from six forty-five to seven in the morning. It came on every morning by the timer on the radio. My family wanted to listen to it together, so the timer was set on the radio in the living room to turn on at the same time as well. We all listened to the series together as we had breakfast and repeated in unison, my father and my mother and I. (laughs) (Tae: So, did you always listen as you had breakfast?) Well, and other things. You see, all the radios in the house were set by timer to turn on at that

> time. So, we could listen to it at the kitchen table, or in the bathroom if we had to go there to brush our teeth. So we could spend our morning doing what people normally do but as we listened and repeated in a loud voice. (Chiaki)

Chiaki's family placed radios in several places in the home so that everyone could listen even if they did not keep the exact regularity of their daily routines. This example shows the effectiveness of this kind of tactic although it is largely dependent on the particular culture of the family.

Another point worth mentioning is that, though four students said they recorded the programmes, they also listened/watched at the time of the broadcast. In other words, the recording was not done for the purpose of allowing flexibility with regard to time constraints, but simply to listen to or watch the broadcast repeatedly after first listening to or watching the original live broadcast. Those students who did not record the programmes, when asked why they did not do so, made clear the importance of not doing so in order to persist, as in the following comments:

> (3) Not recording the programmes is more effective, because when it's the time of broadcast, it's there, so I go and switch on the radio. I feel 'I have to do it today.' If I recorded it, I would probably think 'I can listen to it any time' and never actually do it. (Aiko)

In the above comment, not having control over time is mentioned as an advantage in that, if the programmes had been recorded, students would never actually find time to listen.

Whereas all the Early starters reported they followed the series at a fixed time, three Non-completers said they did not set a fixed time for listening to or watching the series (see extract 4). Two recorded the programmes but did not listen to the recordings at a fixed time. All of the Non-completers reported listening or watching in their own room by themselves and finding difficulties in following the series at the fixed times of the broadcasts:

> (4) The series were either very early in the morning, at midday or in the early evening and it was impossible for me to listen to the series every day at any of these times. (Junko)

### Presence of family

As we have already seen most of the Early starters mentioned the presence and support of their family members. Thus, during the interview with the first participant, I realized that I needed to add the question 'Did you study with anyone else?' to the interview in order to understand the students' learning situations. Figure 10.3 summarizes the time and place of learning, and the support received from the family.

141

| Participant | Time | Recorded | Place | Family |
|---|---|---|---|---|
| **Early starters / Late completers** | | | | |
| Miwako | fixed (evening) | no | kitchen area | mother, sister |
| Motoo | fixed (evening) | no | kitchen area | no support |
| Aiko | fixed (evening) | no | kitchen area | mother |
| Moe | fixed (evening) | yes | own room | mother |
| Noriko | fixed (morning) | no | living room | mother |
| Yasuko | fixed (morning) | no | kitchen area | no support |
| **Early starters / Late non-completers** | | | | |
| Mami | fixed (evening) | no | kitchen area | sister |
| Satoko | fixed (evening) | yes | own room | father |
| Kayo | fixed (evening) | yes | kitchen area | no support |
| Rika | fixed (evening) | yes | living room | no support |
| Chiaki | fixed (morning) | no | kitchen area | mother, father |
| **Non-completers** | | | | |
| Junko | fixed (evening) | no | own room | no support |
| Masuo | fixed (evening) | no | own room | no support |
| Kaori | unfixed | yes | own room | no support |
| Aki | unfixed | no | own room | no support |
| Seiko | unfixed | yes | own room | no support |

Figure 10.3 Time, place of study and family support for students before entering university

As we have seen in extracts (1) and (2) above, some students mentioned they actually listened to or watched the series together with one, or in some cases both, of their parents, and/or with their brother(s) or sister(s). Other students received support from their parents in other ways: by taking the initiative to obtain the textbooks for them, by regularly recording the series for them, by giving them the priority of choosing the programmes on radio and television, and by adjusting mealtimes. The support students received from family was not restricted to physical or material support. More importantly, students often mentioned the encouragement and praise they received from their parents, as we see below:

> (5) I sat at the desk in my room and listened to the series on the radio and repeated after the models. It was around six in the evening. My room was sort of attached to the living room without any walls, so my mother could see me studying. She never repeated together with me or anything but she always recorded the programmes on tape for me when I could not listen to them for some reason. So I have never ever missed a single programme in

my life! Sometimes she would make comments like 'Your pronunciation sounds like a native speaker's.' And my English grades were very high and I was happy. I believed that listening to the series did this. (Aiko)

Also, as observed in extracts (1) and (5), where cases of a so-called 'kyouiku mama' (educational mother, or a mother who is very keen on her children's education) are illustrated, Japanese parents are generally keen on and prioritize children's education due to the importance attached to educational achievement in society. Because this mode of learning takes place in people's homes, this kind of family environment takes on particular importance and appears to have influenced the learning process for the Early starters. On the other hand, the Non-completers reported having followed the series in their own bedroom, in isolation, and did not report receiving support from their family (Figure 10.3). Junko in extract (4), for example, may have been able to persist if her family had recorded the programmes for her. This isolation and lack of family support could be a significant factor in explaining their withdrawal.

## Learning with broadcast materials during university

Let us now turn to the learning circumstances of students in their university years. Ten students (six Early starters and four Late starters) have completed one or more broadcast courses during university. As described earlier, the Early starters / Late completers had already started using the broadcast materials in their schooldays, and by the time of entering university had already had extended experiences using the materials. On the other hand, the Late starters had started using broadcast materials comparatively recently. One focus will be to see whether this difference in experience might be related to differences in any of the areas of concern.

### The regularity of time and place of learning

Considerable differences were observed in the learning environments of university students compared to those before they entered university. Generally, students reported studying in their own room rather than in the kitchen area or living room, and studying on their own rather than with family members (see Figure 10.4). This was also due to the fact that the students had moved out of their parents' homes and started living on their own in order to go to university. In one case, Chiaki from the Early starters / Late non-completers group reported that this change in living environment was the major cause for her not being able to continue with the series she had attempted to pursue just after she started at university:

143

| Participant | Time | Recorded | Place | Family |
|---|---|---|---|---|
| **Early starters / Late completers** | | | | |
| Miwako | fixed (night) | no | own room | no support |
| Motoo | fixed (night) | no | own room | no support |
| Aiko | fixed (night) | no | own room | mother |
| Moe | fixed (night) | yes | own room | no support |
| Noriko | unfixed (morning) | yes | own room | no support |
| Yasuko | fixed (morning) | yes | own room | no support |
| **Late starters** | | | | |
| Ryoko | fixed (morning) | yes | own room | no support |
| Ikuyo | fixed (evening) | yes | own room | no support |
| Mitsuyo | fixed (evening) | yes | own room /bathroom | no support |
| Kouichi | fixed (morning) | no | living room | no support |
| **Non-completers** | | | | |
| Junko | fixed (night) | no | living room | mother |
| Masuo | unfixed | yes | own room | no support |
| Kaori | unfixed | yes | own room | no support |
| Aki | unfixed | yes | own room | no support |
| * Seiko in this group did not report pursuing any course during these years | | | | |

Figure 10.4 Time, place of study and family support for students during university

> (6) I could not listen to the radio series any more like I used to do every morning. (Tae: Why was that?) I don't know. I did not know how to set the timer on my radio to come on in the morning. (Laughs) Maybe because I was on my own. Before, we used to listen together as a family and that helped a great deal. When I went to my parents' home this past summer, the radio was still set to come on at 6:30 [am]. I got nostalgic. (Chiaki)

Furthermore, differences were observed between the Early starters and the Late starters in the manner in which they pursued the series. The six Early starters / Late completers persisted in listening to or watching the series at the time of the broadcast as they had done in earlier years. By the time they entered university, they had already 'habitualized' the act of following the broadcast materials and they reported no difficulty in keeping up their studies although they did not receive as much support from their families as before and studied individually. They not only found few difficulties in persisting, but some even mentioned that not listening or watching made them feel uneasy:

(7) Listening to the radio language courses has become habitualized. When it is 10:40, which is the time of the broadcast, I get restless wherever I am. I feel strange not to listen to the radio around that time. (Motoo)

On the other hand, the Late completers who started listening to / watching the series when their lives were more complicated needed different tactics to persist, such as recording the programmes onto tapes to listen to on the train during commuting or in bed, and listening to the broadcast while taking a bath:

(8) My apartment subscribes to a special cable channel solely devoted to language courses. It's great 'cause they play the same programme over and over again, so I can switch on the radio just like that and listen to it whenever I like. This enabled me to continue studying with the radio series. It's been very useful. My mother doesn't like it being on, because she doesn't understand foreign languages and she says it drives her crazy. So, I started listening to it early in the morning when I am having a bath . . . there is a speaker in the bathroom, I don't know why. (Tae: But don't you look at your textbook?) Well, I look at it as I get ready. And then in the bath tub, I just listen and repeat in a small voice, otherwise my neighbours will hear me and they'll think I'm strange. (Mitsuyo)

Such creativity is understandable considering the potential irregularity of university students' lifestyles. Nonetheless, the Late starters persisted in listening to / watching the recordings at a fixed time of the day. This makes for a contrast with the Non-completers, who tended not to set a fixed time for listening to or watching the series.

### Goal setting

Another factor which enabled students to continue may lie in the ways they set their goals in relation to the courses. Again, an interesting difference can be observed between the Early starters and the Late starters.

The Early starters tended not to have a clear purpose in pursuing the courses. Their goal was rather continuing itself as they seemed to believe strongly in the 'power of continuing'. To that end, they deliberately did not try hard and 'took it easy':

(9) I take it easy. If I think like 'I have to try hard, I'm going to get better', I will probably get tired and may quit. But even if I cannot catch what they are saying, I say to myself, 'I'll come to catch it one day.' (Aiko)

In contrast, the Late starters tended to describe their learning in relation to explicit goals, such as studying abroad, studying for exams or studying their major language. And because of this they reported a variety of creative ways they had invented for using the materials, such as transcribing the dialogues or simply concentrating on the functional expressions, making a clear contrast to the Early starters who deliberately did not make special effort. On the other hand, the Non-completers also tended to have no clear purpose for studying with broadcast courses.

> (10) I started watching this series, because I felt I should do something. I generally feel that I should do something to improve my English. But then it got tiresome. When there were other programmes I wanted to watch on TV, I tended to watch those instead of the series. I felt a bit guilty but kept watching. (Aki)

## Discussion

The investigation allowed us to gain insights into areas of self-instructional learning which could not have been revealed by large-scale close-ended surveys. Let us summarize our findings as we point out their implications.

Through the study, we identified some factors which seem to contribute to persistence in learning with broadcast materials. First, the study points to the importance of routine setting, as has also been suggested by Jones (1996). Learners who persisted tended to listen to / watch the series at a fixed time, pace and place, either by attending to the series at the time of the broadcast or setting a different time to listen to / watch the recordings. This contrasts with the Non-completers, who tended not to have a fixed time or pace of learning. The ease with which routines can be set with broadcast materials has already been indicated in the questionnaire study (Figure 10.1), thus confirming the relative advantage of broadcast materials over other types of self-instructional materials in this respect (Umino 1999).

Secondly, learners who persisted, particularly at a younger age, tended to report receiving support from their family in one form or another. Learners often attend to the series with other family members, naturally forming a 'self-help group' (Rybak 1983) which prevented them from being isolated and enhanced the enjoyment. Family members also purchased textbooks for the learner, adjusted mealtimes so as not to overlap with the broadcasts, recorded the programmes when the learner could not attend to them and provided encouragement and praise. The Non-completers did not receive such support and worked in isolation.

While the above discussion supports Rybak's (1983) argument that 'isolation' is a factor responsible for dropout, it also suggests that the types of support needed for home learners may differ depending on the cultural group to which they belong. Learners learning within the naturally formed family self-help groups as reported in this study, for example, do not require further support in this area.

This point also highlights the influence of the culture of the family within a home, which becomes of particular relevance since this type of learning takes place in one's home. The particular ways in which the rooms in a house are structured, the types of daily routines a family goes through, or the relationships they have amongst themselves can all influence how learners go about attending to the series and whether they will be able to maintain it. This influence of a home-culture has not been addressed in the literature on self-instruction, but is certainly a factor contributing to success and failure of this mode of learning. This also suggests an important perspective for research into distance learning, which also tends to take place in one's home, although this was not the focus of the present study.

The study also indicated that the tactics required for persistence may vary depending on the age of the learners and the goals they set for themselves. Learners at a younger age, particularly in junior high school, tend to follow a fairly regular lifestyle, which is advantageous for routine setting. But as they get older and their lifestyles become more irregular, different tactics may be needed to cope with this irregularity. This may be one area in which adult learners require support. Furthermore, learners who did not have specific goals for learning with the series and simply believed in the power of continuing deliberately made little effort so as not to burden the process, whereas learners who had specific short-term goals attempted to make use of the materials in creative ways. Thus, learners may need to clarify their goals before deciding on tactics for using the materials.

This third point raises an interesting issue regarding the relationship between effort and persistence. If we consider the above two types of learners in terms of persistence and intensity (Kanfer and Ackerman 1989), the Early starters / Late completers managed to maintain their effort over a long period of time by dispensing with its intensity whereas the Late starters could pursue the task with intensity only by setting a relatively short-term span. This implies that amount of effort may be in a contradictory relationship with persistence. Moreover, the findings run counter to suggestions that learners with specific and challenging goals persist longer at a task than those with vague goals (Locke and Latham 1990). Thus, there is a need to investigate further the relationships between effort, goal setting and persistence.

The findings of the study can also be discussed in the light of learner control in self-instruction. In the context of learner autonomy, learners engaged in materials-centred self-instruction have often been viewed as passive beings who simply follow decisions made by the materials designers rather than taking control of their learning (for example, Holec 1979). However, the persisting learners in this study deliberately submitted themselves to these externally made decisions in order to create order and organization in this pressure-free mode of learning. In other words, the deliberate abandonment of control was used as a strategy for persistence. This resonates with Jones' (1996) finding that 'well-structured' self-instructional materials were appreciated by his subjects. These findings indicate the need to reconsider the role of structure in self-instructional materials and to look further into the complex relationship between materials and learners in further discussing the issue of learner control in self-instruction.

Finally, this study has made use of narrative data of learners' past learning experiences, or 'recollective data' (Cohen 1998), obtained by means of semi-structured interviews. By constructing learners' 'learning histories' with this data, it has been possible to identify certain patterns in the use of broadcast materials in terms of age of starting and length of study which seemed to correspond to certain types of needs learners have for learning with broadcast materials. And this also indicated that learners' past learning experiences affect the ways learners use the materials at present. Such insights could not have been gained if we only collected data on the learners' present learning situations.

## Conclusion

This chapter has focused on interviews with 20 Japanese university students on their experiences of L2 learning with broadcast materials. Employment of an exploratory approach has enabled us to shed light on some of the factors which play a role in making persistence possible in L2 self-instruction and has contributed to an understanding of the nature of self-instruction more generally.

The present study focused mainly on social-environmental factors within the home which enabled the students to persist. However, there are other areas which need to be investigated in order to understand this issue fully. For example, although the study indicated that the materials have an effect on learners' incentives to persist, it is still unclear what features of the materials are important in this respect. Nor did I investigate motivational aspects which may explain the differences in the approaches between different types of learners. Furthermore, while the use of 'recollective data' was advantageous in introducing an angle of learning histories, thus enabling us to identify different patterns in the use of broadcast materials, it does not allow us to understand how the task of persistence is dealt with in their daily learning endeavours. To capture this aspect, a longitudinal or dynamic study (Block 1995a), using in-depth observational and self-report data-gathering techniques, would be needed. More research along these lines would help us better understand the complex process of self-instruction and persistence.

## Notes

1. 'Dropping out' is used here to refer to 'stopping a given course before reaching the end of it'. Jones (1996) distinguishes 'dropout', that is, 'stopping before one's aims have been met', from 'retirement', that is, 'stopping after one's aims have been met'. The act of stopping itself may be variably motivated, as pointed out by Jones, but whether or not a learner stopped before completing a course is objectively identifiable and serves as a useful measure in considering the problem of persistence. Accordingly, 'retirement' and 'dropout' will not be differentiated here.
2. Most Early starters started their broadcast courses in English at age 13. This corresponds to the introduction of English in junior high school. The foreign language introduced in junior high or high schools need not be English but in reality English is taught in the majority of schools. Also, in some schools, English may be introduced at the elementary school level.
3. From students' descriptions, it seems that a small television or radio is often placed in this area. This also seems to be where family members generally get together.

# 11    Conclusion

*David Nunan and Phil Benson*

This volume is based on a collection of learners' accounts of the processes involved in their language learning. While the theme of difference and diversity emerges and re-emerges throughout the collection, the principal aim is to make a case for (auto)biography as a legitimate research genre, and to demonstrate the genre in action, through a range of analyses of these accounts. In this concluding chapter, we would therefore like to address some of the methodological and substantive issues and perspectives that emerge from the various contributions and inform the volume as a whole. We begin with the methodological issue of (auto)biography as a research genre before moving on to summarize the key substantive issues raised by each chapter. In the final section, we present three observations that we believe provide thematic unity to these chapters.

## Revisiting (auto)biography as research

The principal methodological aim of this collection is to advance the case of (auto)biography as a legitimate research genre within the qualitative research paradigm. We acknowledge that the distinction between qualitative and quantitative research can be simplistic and naïve and that the two traditions are not mutually exclusive. Indeed, studies drawing on both traditions are appearing in the literature with increasing frequency. Nonetheless, we believe that the distinction is a real one and can be useful as a way of thinking about, understanding and representing the world around us. As Nunan (1992, p. 10) has written:

> One reason for the persistence of the distinction between quantitative and qualitative research is that the two approaches represent different ways of thinking about and understanding the world around us. Underlying the development of different research traditions and methods is a debate on the nature of knowledge and the status of assertions about the world, and the debate itself is ultimately a philosophical one.

At issue here is the status of knowledge, and what counts as legitimate data for research. (Auto)biographies are a form of storytelling and stories are increasingly recognized as a legitimate way of knowing the world. As Denny (1978) argues, in defence of storytelling as a legitimate form of research, stories, like ethnographies and case studies, provide a portrait of what is going on in a particular setting. However, they are more than mere 'objective' accounts – they go beyond description and present a point of view. He also argues that they should be rich enough to enable the reader 'to draw conclusions other than those presented directly by the writer' (Nunan 1992, p. 77).

Stenhouse (1983), one of the champions of illuminative research in education, provides an equally telling argument for the use of stories in research:

> The important point about the illuminative tradition is that it . . . aimed to appeal to professional judgement. . . . From this desire to appeal to professional judgement comes a range of concerns about presentation and about audiences. In particular, there is a need to capture in the presentation of the research the texture of reality which makes judgement possible for an audience. This cannot be achieved in the reduced, attenuated accounts of events which support quantification. The contrast is between the breakdown of questionnaire responses of 472 women respondents who have had affairs with men other than their husbands and the novel *Madam Bovary*. The novel relies heavily on that appeal to judgement which is appraisal of credibility in the light of the reader's experience. You cannot base much appeal to judgement on the statistics of survey; the portrayal relies almost entirely upon appeal to judgement.
>
> (Stenhouse 1983, pp. 2–3)

This quote from Stenhouse articulates perfectly the (auto)biographical perspective that emerges in this volume. As we indicated in the Introduction, its chapters are less concerned with establishing causal relationships between psychological and social variables and differential proficiency outcomes than with providing holistic descriptions of the development of difference and diversity over time. Such descriptions necessarily focus on psychological and social factors, but these are always viewed within the context of learners' broader life circumstances and goals.

Within the second language learning literature, there is a tension between the search for universals and the goal of generalizability, on the one hand, and the identification of diversity and the goal of insight, on the other. Much of the mainstream SLA research seeks to make generalizable statements about processes of acquisition, morphosyntactic developmental sequences and so on. There is also a rich literature on individual learner differences investigating a range of variables (for a review, see Ellis 1994). Most of these studies seek to establish some kind of relationship between individual differences and learning outcomes such as proficiency, achievement and rate of acquisition. While the studies reported in this volume document the role of factors of motivation, affect, age, beliefs and strategies, identity and setting, they are concerned less with establishing causality than with presenting descriptive and interpretive portraits of the inter-relationships between psychosocial phenomena and with the ways these inter-relationships develop over the longer term.

## The studies: Methodological and substantive issues

In this section we gloss each of the contributions to the volume and use these summaries to draw out thematic threads running through the stories that lie at the heart of each study. Although we have not divided this volume into sections, the chapters fall naturally into two different groups: those with a psychological orientation (Chapters 3 to 7) and those that look at the role of settings for learning in language development.

Shoaib and Dörnyei (Chapter 3) identify how motivational influences on the learning process develop over time and document events and factors that can prompt a restructuring of learners' motivational dispositions. Methodologically, their research differs from most motivational studies in that motivational factors are distilled from real-life learning experiences rather than through elicitation by way of questionnaires or self-report inventories. Substantively, they found that motivation is an inherently unstable construct that fluctuates over time, and they identified a variety of factors that had both positive and negative impacts on the participants in the study. Methodologically, they affirm the value of learners' stories because they enable phenomena that are usually studied in isolation to be investigated in context.

So and Domínguez (Chapter 4) provide an oral narrative of the experience of one of the authors (Domínguez) acquiring English as a graduate student in the United States. The database for the study is a series of recorded conversations between the two authors on this experience. Analysis of the transcripts of the conversations revealed the centrality and power of emotion in the learning process. So and Domínguez point out that, although the importance of affective factors to second language learning has long been recognized (see, for example, Schmidt 1983), quantitative research methods are inappropriate for documenting emotion as a process (rather than a state) and that an alternative research paradigm incorporating learning histories and oral narratives is needed. As a result of their study, the authors suggest that future inquiry might focus on the issue of how a balance between reason and emotion might be achieved in order to 'motivate and sustain action directed towards long-term objectives'.

Age as a factor in second language learning is a recurring theme in the literature. While most research has focused on the notion of a critical period, and the optimal age for beginning a foreign language, there is also some interest in the question of the extent to which older individuals can successfully acquire a foreign language. This issue is attracting increasing attention with globalization and the increasing mobility of professionals and paraprofessionals as well as the ongoing needs of older immigrants and refugees. In her descriptive account of the experiences of five Asian learners of English, Bellingham (Chapter 5) chooses to focus on the learners' beliefs and experiences and the contexts of their learning. As with other studies in the collection, she finds that the learners' stories illuminate a reality that transcends the language learning process itself. One of the striking things about the learner profiles presented in her chapter is the fact that, despite the biographical similarities between the learners, their attitudes, learning preferences and approaches to learning are quite diverse. This diversity notwithstanding, one common theme that emerged from all informants was that with the right attitude, learning could be successful regardless of chronological age. Other shared themes were the amount of time needed in order for progress to be evident and the importance of confidence and self-esteem.

A strong theme emerging from Malcolm's study of the development of autonomy on the part of an Arabic learner of English (Chapter 6) is the inherent instability of learners' belief systems. As with other studies in this collection, the elongated time frame of the interviews enables her to generate insights that are simply not available through the more usual 'snapshot' studies that deploy one-off questionnaire and interview data. As Malcolm notes, a study of her informant, Hamad, as a first-year university learner would have yielded a very different image from the Hamad who emerges at the end of the study. Hamad's voice provides dramatic evidence of the changing interplay between learner beliefs and action as he seeks to find strategies for becoming an effective reader, and to operationalize his conviction that learning through reading was the best way for him to acquire English.

Murphey, Chen and Chen (Chapter 7) present the results of an ambitious investigation into learner-constructed identity and imagined communities based on 84 Japanese and 58 Taiwanese language learning histories. The investigators used a guided report format in which informants constructed their histories by responding to ten questions posed by the investigators. As with a number of other contributions to the volume, the researchers find that the self-reported, longitudinal experiences display considerable instability and change over time. The construct of an 'imagined community' is an intriguing one in the context of language learning. In an EFL situation, for learners who lack an imagined community with which to identify and invest their language learning efforts, that target language will remain a subject for formal study for the purposes of passing examinations rather than become a tool for communication in some actual or potential future situation. The Murphey, Chen and Chen study provides interesting insights into events that lead to learner investment and identification as well as de-investment and de-identification. The roles of significant others – friends, fellow students, family members and teachers in particular – appear to have a powerful influence on investment and identification. This point resonates strongly with other recently published studies based on language learning histories (see, for example, Benson and Nunan 2002).

The final three studies place instructional setting under the lens. Cotterall's study (Chapter 8) is set in the classroom, Sataporn and Lamb (Chapter 9) in a distance learning setting and Umino (Chapter 10) in self-instructional environments.

In the introduction to her case study of a beginning adult learner of Spanish, Cotterall foregrounds the tension between reporting the experiences of the individual and generalizing from the individual account to a population of learners. Explicitly disclaiming the generalizability of her account, Cotterall argues that the general is nothing more that the accumulation of individual instances. Her study is justified as the contribution of an instance in action to a growing body of related instances, several of which are reported in this volume. She is also able to link insights from her study to other research, such as that by Slimani (1989), which claimed priority of learner agendas over teacher agendas. One of the major themes to emerge from this collection (and one that is expanded upon later in this chapter) is the intimate connection between what is happening inside the classroom and everything else that is going on in an individual's life. This theme is dramatized in Cotterall's study, which clearly shows her subject attempting to fit classroom language learning 'into his broader perspective of learning and into his life'.

Sataporn and Lamb present case studies of two students studying language at a distance. The cases are drawn from a larger group of 36 distance learners studying at a higher education institute in Thailand. The focus of the study is the well-documented high attrition rates in distance learning programmes. The researchers describe the success of one informant (in terms of completing the course) and the failure of the other in terms of 'accommodation zones'. The more successful learner was able to create an accommodation zone between his personal culture and the culture of the programme (culture being used here in its broadest sense as sets of rules and norms for action and living). The other was unable to create such a zone. Again, as with other studies in the collection, we see a dynamic tension between the learning process and everyday life. It may well be that the high attrition rates from distance programmes is a direct result of the greater difficulty in creating separate learning spaces, or accommodation zones, between formal learning and everyday life than is the case in face-to-face learning contexts.

Umino, the final contributor to the collection, also explores the challenges of learning a foreign language outside of a formal learning environment. Like several other studies in the collection, this one provides a longitudinal perspective on what goes on as learners pursue self-instruction at home. Unlike the preceding study of distance learning, the informants in this study are attempting to learn outside of an institutionalized educational system using materials that are broadcast through the radio. The aim of Umino's study is to gain insights into those factors at play in determining learner persistence in self-instructional contexts. From the study, Umino concluded that a fixed time and pace of learning facilitated persistence as did familial support. In fact the 'culture of the home' emerged as particularly important for persistence – hardly surprising, as the home was where the learning took place.

## Some observations

In this section we offer some observations on the studies summarized in the preceding section. We hesitate to call these observations 'generalizations'. However, we invite the reader to contest the learners' stories on which these studies are based against the realities of their own experiences as language teachers and learners. Following Stenhouse (1983), we and our fellow contributors have tried to capture in these learners' stories the 'texture of reality' which will enable the reader to make judgements in the light of their own experiences, and to draw their own conclusions.

### Observation 1: Language learning and attitudes towards language learning are unstable and change over time

One of the distinguishing features of (auto)biographical research is that it offers a longitudinal portrait of the phenomena under investigation. This enables us to generate insights that are beyond the reach of 'snapshot' research which captures a single reality, or a limited number of realities, at a single point in time. A common thread running through most of the accounts in this volume is that language learning practices and attitudes towards learning are unstable and change over time. In other words, difference and diversity exist not just between learners, but within learners at different stages of their language learning experience. The question at issue is not simply how and why learners differ from each other. It is also a matter of how their differences emerge as their learning progresses over time.

*Observation 2: Learner difference is a complex construct*

The fact that learners are different and learn in different ways is a major theme of this volume. The contributions to the volume also show that learner difference is a complex construct that cannot be reduced to the influence of isolated variables. This complexity is particularly brought out through investigation of learners' stories of their experiences. While the studies presented here reflect some of the psychological and social factors that result in, for example, variable learning outcomes, they seek to present an integrated rather than atomistic view of these factors.

*Observation 3: The processes and goals of language learning are intimately interconnected with other aspects of individuals' lives*

This third observation follows from the second. Mainstream approaches to SLA research tend to isolate psychological and social variables such as motivation, affect, age, beliefs and strategies, identity and setting from each other. However, one of the strongest themes to emerge from this collection is that, for learners, these factors are intimately entwined, not just with each other, but with the learners' larger life circumstances and goals.

We anticipate scepticism on the part of some readers toward storytelling as a legitimate form of research. As we noted in the introduction to this collection, the literature is littered with objections to 'subjectivity' in research. Hopefully, however, a reading of this volume will convince the sceptic that the richness of (auto)biographical accounts more than compensates for any perceived deficiencies.

# References

Allen, L. 1996. The evolution of a learner's beliefs about language learning. *Carleton Papers in Applied Linguistics*, 13, 67–80.

Anderson, B. 1991. *Imagined communities: Reflections on the origins and spread of nationalism*. Revised edition. London: Verso.

Aoki, N. 2002. Teachers' conversation with partial autobiographies. *Hong Kong Journal of Applied Linguistics*, 7(2), 152–68.

Arnold, J. (ed.) 1999. *Affect in language learning*. Cambridge: Cambridge University Press.

Bailey, K. M. 1980. An introspective analysis of an individual's language learning experience. In R. C. Scarcella and S. D. Krashen (eds.), *Research in second language acquisition* (pp. 58–65). Rowley, MA: Newbury House.

   1983. Competitiveness and anxiety in adult language second language acquisition: Looking *at* and *through* diary studies. In H. Seliger and M. H. Long (eds.), *Classroom oriented research in second language acquisition* (pp. 123–35). Rowley, MA: Newbury House.

   1991. Diary studies of classroom language learning: The doubting game and the believing game. In E. Sadtono (ed.), *Language acquisition and the second/foreign language classroom* (pp. 60–102). RELC Anthology Series 28. Singapore: RELC.

Bailey, K. M. and Nunan, D. C. 1996. *Voices from the language classroom: Qualitative research in second language education*. Cambridge: Cambridge University Press.

Bailey, K. M. and Ochsner, R. 1983. A methodological review of the diary studies: Windmill tilting or social science? In K. M. Bailey, M. H. Long and S. Peck (eds.), *Second language acquisition studies* (pp. 188–98). Rowley, MA: Newbury House.

Barkhuizen, G. 2004. Social influences on language learning. In A. Davies and C. Elder (eds.), *The handbook of applied linguistics* (pp. 552–75). Oxford: Blackwell.

Bateson, M. 1994. *Peripheral visions*. New York: HarperCollins.

Belcher, D. and Connor, U. (eds.) 2001. *Reflections on multiliterate lives*. Clevedon: Multilingual Matters.

Bell, J. S. 1995. The relationship between L1 and L2 literacy: Some complicating factors. *TESOL Quarterly*, 29, 687–704.

   1997. *Literacy, culture and identity*. New York: Peter Lang.

   2002. Narrative inquiry: More than just telling stories. *TESOL Quarterly*, 36, 207–18.

# References

Benson, P. 2001. *Teaching and researching autonomy in language learning.* Harlow: Pearson Education.

Benson, P., Chik, A. and Lim, H-Y. 2003. Becoming autonomous in an Asian context: Autonomy as a sociocultural process. In D. Palfreyman and R. C. Smith (eds.), *Learner autonomy across cultures* (pp. 23–40). London: Palgrave Macmillan.

Benson, P. and Lor, W. 1998. *Making sense of autonomous language learning: conceptions of learning and readiness for autonomy.* English Centre Monograph No. 2. University of Hong Kong.

Benson, P. and Nunan (eds.), D. 2002. The experience of language learning. Special issue of the *Hong Kong Journal of Applied Linguistics*, 7(2).

2004. *What learners know about learning and using English: A study of the language learning experiences of Hong Kong University students.* English Centre Monograph No. 3. University of Hong Kong.

Bernard, R. and Amundsen, C. 1989. Antecedents to dropout in distance education: Does one fit all? *Distance Education*, 42, 25–46.

Bertaux, D. (ed.) 1981. *Biography and society: The life history approach in the social sciences.* Beverley Hills, CA: Sage.

Bialystok, E. 1994. *In other words.* New York: HarperCollins

Binet, A. and Simon, T. 1973. *The development of intelligence in children: The Binet–Simon scale.* New York: Arno.

Block, D. 1994. A day in the life of a class: Teacher/learner perceptions of task purpose in conflict. *System*, 22(4), 473–86.

1995a. Exploring learners' worlds: Two studies. PhD thesis, Lancaster University.

1995b. Social constraints on interviews. *Prospect*, 10(3), 35–48.

1996a. A window on the classroom: Classroom events viewed from different angles. In K. M. Bailey and D. Nunan (eds.), *Voices from the language classroom* (pp. 168–94). Cambridge: Cambridge University Press.

1996b. Not so fast: Some thoughts on theory culling, relativism, accepted findings and the heart and soul of SLA. *Applied Linguistics*, 17(1), 63–83.

1998. Tale of a language learner. *Language Teaching Research*, 2(2), 148–76.

2000. Problematizing interview data: Voices in the mind's machine? *TESOL Quarterly*, 34, 757–63.

2002. Destabilized identities and cosmopolitanism across language and cultural borders: Two case studies. *Hong Kong Journal of Applied Linguistics*, 7(2), 1–19.

2003. *The social turn in second language acquisition.* Edinburgh: Edinburgh University Press.

Bongaerts, T., van Summeren, C., Planken, B. and Schils, E. 1997. Age and ultimate attainment in the pronunciation of a foreign language. *Studies in Second Language Acquisition*, 19, 447–65.

Booker, L. and Bur, A-M. 1982. *Foreign languages by radio and television: A report on the current research project.* Brighton Polytechnic, Language Centre.

Breen, M. P. 2001. Introduction: Conceptualization, affect, and action in context. In M. P. Breen (ed.), *Learner contributions to language learning* (pp. 1–11). London: Longman.

Brown, H. D. 1990. M&Ms for language classrooms? Another look at motivation. In J. E. Alatis (ed.), *Georgetown University Round Table on Language and Linguistics 1990* (pp. 383–93). Washington, DC: Georgetown University Press.

Brown, T. P. 2002. Auto-communal language learning of Mandarin Chinese and Samoan: A chronicle and comparison. *Hong Kong Journal of Applied Linguistics*, 7(2), 122–35.

Bruner, J. 1990. *Acts of meaning*. Cambridge, MA: Harvard University Press.
1991. The narrative construction of reality. *Critical Inquiry*, 8, 1–21.

Cameron, D. 2000. Difficult subjects. *Critical Quarterly*, 42(4), 89–94.

Campbell, C. 1996. Socializing with the teachers and prior language learning experience: A diary study. In K. M. Bailey and D. Nunan (eds.), *Voices from the language classroom*. (pp. 201–23). Cambridge: Cambridge University Press.

Carter, B-A. 2002. Helping learners come of age: Learner autonomy in a Caribbean context. *Hong Kong Journal of Applied Linguistics*, 7(2), 20–38.

Casanave, C. P. and Schecter, S. R. (eds.) 1997. *On becoming a language educator: Personal essays on professional development*. Mahwah, NJ: Lawrence Erlbaum.

Catford, J. C. 1998. *Language Learning* and applied linguistics: A historical sketch. *Language Learning*, 48(4), 465–96.

Cazden, C., Cancino, H., Rosansky, E. J. and Schumann, J. H. 1975. *Second language acquisition sequences in children, adolescents and adults*. US Department of Health, Education and Welfare.

Chamberlayne, P., Bornat, J. and Wengraf, T. (eds.) 2000. *The turn to biographical methods in social science: Comparative issues and examples*. London: Routledge.

Chen, J. 2002. Commander and serviceman – The story of Kim. *Hong Kong Journal of Applied Linguistics*, 7(2), 73–90.

Ciarrochi, J., Chan, A., Caputi, P. and Roberts, R. 2001. Measuring emotional intelligence. In J. Ciarrochi, J. P. Forgas and J. D. Mayer (eds.), *Emotional intelligence in everyday life: A scientific inquiry* (pp. 25–45). Philadelphia: Psychology Press.

Clandinin, D. J. and Connelly, M. F. 1994. Personal experience methods. In N. K. Denzin and Y. S. Lincoln (eds.), *Handbook of qualitative research* (pp. 413–27). Thousand Oaks, CA: Sage.

Clarke, M. A. 2003. *A place to stand*. Ann Arbor: University of Michigan Press.

Clément, R. and Gardner, R. C. 2001. Second language mastery. In W. P. Robinson and H. Giles (eds.), *The new handbook of language and social psychology* (pp. 489–504). Chichester: Wiley and Sons.

Cohen, A. D. 1998. *Strategies in learning and using a second language*. London: Longman.

Cohen, A. D. and Scott, K. 1996. A synthesis of approaches to assessing language learning strategies. In R. L. Oxford (ed.), *Language learning strategies around the world: Cross-cultural perspectives* (pp. 89–106). Honolulu: University of Hawaii.

Connor, U. 1999. Learning to write academic prose in a second language: A literacy autobiography. In G. Braine (ed.), *Non-native educators in English language teaching* (pp. 29–42). Mahwah, NJ: Lawrence Erlbaum.

Cook, V. 1995. Multi-competence and effects of age. In D. Singleton and Z. Lengyel (eds.), *The age factor in second language acquisition* (pp. 51–66). Clevedon: Multilingual Matters.

1999. Going beyond the native speaker in language teaching. *TESOL Quarterly*, 33(2), 185–209.

Covington, M. V. 1998. *The will to learn: A guide for motivating young people.* Cambridge: Cambridge University Press.

Crabtree, B. F. and Miller, W. L. 1992. A template approach to text analysis: Developing and using codebooks. In B. F. Crabtree and W. L. Miller (eds.), *Doing qualitative research* (pp. 93–109). Newbury Park, CA: Sage.

Crookes, G. and Schmidt, R. 1991. Motivation: Reopening the research agenda. *Language Learning*, 41, 469–512.

Deci, E. L. and Ryan, R. M. 1985. *Intrinsic motivation and self-determination in human behavior.* New York: Plenum.

Denny, T. 1978. *Story-telling and educational understanding.* No. 12 Occasional Paper Series, College of Education, Western Michigan University. Reprinted in L. Bartelett, S. Kemmis and G. Gillard (eds.), *Perspectives on case study: The quasi-historical approach.* Geelong Victoria: Deakin University Press.

Denzin, N. K. 1989. *Interpretive biography.* Newbury Park, CA: Sage.

Dewey, J. 1938/1963. *Experience and education* [The Kappa Delta Pi Lecture series]. New York: Macmillan.

Dickinson, L. 1987. *Self-instruction in language learning.* Cambridge: Cambridge University Press.

Dörnyei, Z. 1994. Motivation and motivating in the foreign language classroom. *Modern Language Journal*, 78, 273–84.

1998. Motivation in second and foreign language learning. *Language Teaching*, 78, 117–35.

2000. Motivation in action: Towards a process-oriented conceptualisation of student motivation. *British Journal of Educational Psychology*, 70, 519–38.

2001a. *Teaching and researching motivation.* Harlow: Longman.

2001b. *Motivational strategies in the language classroom.* Cambridge: Cambridge University Press.

Dörnyei, Z. and Ottó, I. 1998. Motivation in action: A process model of L2 motivation. *Working Papers in Applied Linguistics*, 4, 43–69.

Dörnyei, Z. and Skehan, P. 2003. Individual differences in second language learning. In C. J. Doughty and M. H. Long (eds.), *The handbook of second language acquisition* (pp. 589–630). Oxford: Blackwell.

Eckart, H. 1995. Intensive language courses and the adult learner. *Language Learning Journal*, 12, 31–4.

Ehrman, M. 1996. *Understanding second language difficulties.* Thousand Oaks, CA: Sage Publications.

Ehrman, M. and Oxford, R. 1995. Cognition plus: Correlates of language learning success. *Modern Language Journal*, 79(1), 67–89.

Ellis, C. and Bochner, A. P. 2000. Autoethnography, personal narrative, reflexivity. In N. K. Denzin and Y. S. Lincoln. (eds.), *Handbook of qualitative research*. 2nd edition (pp. 733–68). Thousand Oaks, CA: Sage Publications.

Ellis, R. 1990. *Instructed second language acquisition*. 1st edition. Oxford: Blackwell.

1994. *The study of second language acquisition*. Oxford: Oxford University Press.

1999. Theoretical perspectives on interaction and language learning. In R. Ellis (ed.), *Learning a second language through interaction* (pp. 3–31). Amsterdam: John Benjamins.

2004. Individual differences in second language learning. In A. Davies and C. Elder (eds.), *The handbook of applied linguistics* (pp. 525–51). Oxford: Blackwell.

Evans, C. 1988. *Language people: The experience of teaching and learning modern languages in British universities*. Milton Keynes: Open University Press.

Firth, A. and Wagner, J. 1997. On discourse, communication and some fundamental concepts in SLA research. *Modern Language Journal*, (81), 285–300.

Flavell, R. and Fearn, S. 1995. *The evaluation of a BBC English radio course in Russia*, January–June. BBC English, Research Report.

Flavell, R. and Micallef, R. 1995. *Learning English by radio: The Mozambique project*. BBC English in association with ESOL Department, Institute of Education, University of London, Research Report.

Freeman, D. 1994. Knowing into doing: Teacher education and the problem of transfer. In D. Li, D. Mahoney and J. Richards (eds.), *Exploring second language teacher development* (pp. 1–20). Hong Kong: City University of Hong Kong.

Fries, S. 1998. Different phases: A personal case study in language adjustment and children's bilingualism. *International Journal of the Sociology of Language*, 13(3), 129–41.

Gao Y-H., Li L-C and Lü J. 2001. Trends in research methods in applied linguistics: China and the West. *English for Specific Purposes*, 20, 1–14.

Gardner, H. 1983. *Frames of mind: The theory of multiple intelligences*. New York: Basic Books.

2000. *The disciplined mind: Beyond facts and standardized tests, the K-12 education that every child deserves*. New York: Penguin Group.

Gardner, R. C. 1985. *Social psychology and second language learning: The role of attitudes and motivation*. London: Edward Arnold.

1997. Individual differences and second language learning. In R. G. Tucker and D. Corson (eds.), *Encyclopedia of language and education*. Volume IV: *Second language education* (pp. 33–42). Amsterdam: Kluwer Academic.

2001. Integrative motivation and second language acquisition. In Z. Dörnyei and R. Schmidt (eds.), *Motivation and second language learning* (pp. 1–20). Honolulu: University of Hawaii Press.

Gardner, R. C. and Lambert, W. E. 1959. Motivational variables in second language acquisition. *Canadian Journal of Psychology*, 13, 266–72.

1972. *Attitudes and motivation in second language learning*. Rowley, MA: Newbury House.

## References

Gardner, R. C. and MacIntyre, P. D. 1991. An instrumental motivation in language study: Who says it isn't effective? *Studies in Second Language Acquisition*, 13, 57–72.

   1993. A student contribution to second language acquisition. *Language Teaching*, 26, 1–11.

Gardner, R. C. and Tremblay, P. F. 1994. On motivation: Measurement and conceptual considerations. *Modern Language Journal*, 78, 524–7.

Gardner, R. C., Tremblay, P. F. and Masgoret, A-M. 1997. Towards a full model of second language learning: An empirical investigation. *Modern Language Journal*, 81, 344–62.

Gee, J. P. 1996. *Social linguistics and literacies*. London: Taylor and Francis.

Giddens, A. 1991. *Modernity and self-identity: Self and society in the late modern age*. Stanford, CA: Stanford University Press.

Gillette, B. 1994. The role of learner goals in L2 success. In J. P. Lantolf and M. Appel (eds.), *Vygotskyan approaches to second language research* (pp. 195–213). Norwood, NJ: Ablex.

Golden-Biddle, K. and Locke, K. 1997. *Composing qualitative research*. Thousand Oaks, CA: Sage.

Goleman, D. 1995. *Emotional intelligence*. New York: Bantam Books.

Goodley, D., Lawthorm, R., Clough, P. and Moore, M. 2004. *Researching life stories: Method, theory, and analyses in a biographical age*. London: RoutledgeFalmer.

Goodson, I. and Sikes, P. 2001. *Life history research in educational settings: Learning from lives*. Buckingham, UK: Open University Press.

Gross, J. J. 1998. The emerging field of emotion regulation: An integrative review. *Review of General Psychology*, 2, 271–99.

Hara, Y. 1992. Kouza bangumi wa dono you ni riyou sareteiru ka sono 3. – riyousha no purofiiru (How are educational broadcasts used 3: The profiles of users as observed in the survey of use of educational broadcasts). NHK monthly report on broadcast research, February, 50–7.

Hasan, R. 1996. Literacy, everyday talk and society. In R. Hasan and G. Williams (eds.), *Literacy in society* (pp. 377–424). New York: Longman.

Hawkins, E. W., Howson, B. and Green, P. 1976. *York evaluation of BBC language courses: 'Ensemble' interim report*. University of York Language Teaching Centre.

   1977. *Report on the 'Sur le vif' evaluation project*. University of York Language Teaching Centre.

   1978. *Report on the 'Allez France!' evaluation project*. University of York Language Teaching Centre.

He A-E. 2002. Learning English in different linguistic and socio-cultural contexts. *Hong Kong Journal of Applied Linguistics*, 7(2), 107–21.

Heckhausen, H. 1991. *Motivation and action*. New York: Springer.

Heckhausen, H. and Kuhl, J. 1985. From wishes to action: The dead ends and short cuts on the long way to action. In M. Frese and J. Sabini (eds.), *Goal-directed behaviour: The concept of action in psychology* (pp. 134–59). London: Lawrence Erlbaum.

Heckhausen, J. 2000. Developmental regulation across the life span: An action-phase model of engagement and disengagement with developmental goals. In J. Heckhausen (ed.), *Motivational psychology of human development: Developing motivation and motivating development* (pp. 213–31). Amsterdam: Elsevier.

Hickey, D. T. 1997. Motivation and contemporary socio-constructivist instructional perspectives. *Educational Psychologist*, 32, 175–93.

Hill, B. 1976. *Report on the 'Wegweiser' research project*. Brighton Polytechnic Language Centre.

1978a. *Report on the 'Ochen Priyatno' BBC FE radio*. Brighton Polytechnic Language Centre.

1978b. *Report on the FE radio 'Get by in French' and 'Get by in Spanish' series*. Brighton Polytechnic Language Centre.

Hill, B. and Truscott, S. 1979. *Report on the 'Digame!' research project*. Brighton Polytechnic Language Centre.

Hinton, L. 2001. Involuntary language loss among immigrants: Asian-American linguistic autobiographies. In J. E. Alatis and A. H. Tan (eds.), *Georgetown University roundtable on languages and linguistics 99* (pp. 203–52). Washington, DC: Georgetown University Press.

Hoffman, E. 1989. *Lost in translation: A life in a new language*. London: Penguin.

Holec, H. 1979. *Autonomy for language learning*. Oxford: Pergamon.

Horwitz, E. K. 1987. Surveying student beliefs about language learning. In A. L. Wenden and J. Rubin (eds.), *Learner strategies in language learning* (pp. 119–29). London: Prentice Hall.

Horwitz, E. K., Breslau, B., Dryden, M. A., Yu, J. F. and McClendon, M. E. 1997. A graduate course focusing on the second language learner. *Modern Language Journal*, 81, 518–26.

Horwitz, E. K., Hsieh, P-H., Bonzo, J. D., Huang, D., Na, Y-H. and Rubrecht, B. G. 2004. Studies of language learners as a tool for helping teachers understand the experience of language learning. *Hong Kong Journal of Applied Linguistics*, 9(2).

Horwitz, E. K. and Young, D. J. 1991. *Language anxiety: From theory and research to classroom implications*. Englewood Cliffs, NJ: Prentice Hall.

Hurd, S. 1998. Too carefully led or too carelessly left alone? *Language Learning Journal* 17, 70–4.

Husman, J. and Lens, W. 1999. The role of the future in student motivation. *Educational Psychologist*, 34, 113–25.

Hyltenstam, K. and Abrahamsson, N. 2001. Comments on S. H. Marinova-Todd, D. B. Marshall and C. E. Snow's 'Three misconceptions about age and L2 learning' – Age and L2 learning: The hazards of matching practical 'implications' with theoretical 'facts'. *TESOL Quarterly*, 35(1), 151–70.

Jespersen, O. 1904. *How to teach a foreign language*. London: George Allen and Unwin.

Johnson, K. E. and Golombek, P. R. 2002. *Teachers' narrative inquiry as professional development*. Cambridge: Cambridge University Press.

Jones, F. R. 1994. The lone language learner: A diary study. *System*, 22, 441–54.

1996. Going it alone: Self-instruction in adult foreign-language learning. PhD thesis, Newcastle University.

1998. Self-instruction and success: A learner-profile study. *Applied Linguistics* 19(3), 378–406.

Josselson, R. and Lieblich, A. (eds.) 1993. *The narrative study of lives*. Newbury Park, CA: Sage.

Julkunen, K. 1989. *Situation- and task-specific motivation in foreign-language learning and teaching*. Joensuu: University of Joensuu.

Kanfer, R. and Ackerman, P. L. 1989. Motivation and cognitive abilities: An integrative/aptitude-treatment interaction approach to skill acquisition. *Journal of Applied Psychology Monograph*, 74, 657–90.

Kanno, Y. 2000. Bilingualism and identity: The stories of Japanese returnees. *International Journal of Bilingual Education and Bilingualism*, 31, 1–18.

2003. *Negotiating bilingual and bicultural identities: Japanese returnees betwixt two worlds*. Mahwah, NJ: Lawrence Erlbaum.

Kaplan, A. 1993. *French lessons: A memoir*. Chicago: University of Chicago Press.

1994. On language memoir. In A. Bammer (ed.), *Displacements: Cultural identities in question* (pp. 59–70). Bloomington: Indiana University Press.

Karniol, R. and Ross, M. 1996. The motivational impact of temporal focus: Thinking about the future and the past. *Annual Review of Psychology*, 47, 593–620.

Kasper, G. 1997. 'A' stands for acquisition: A response to Firth and Wagner. *Modern Language Journal*, 81(3), 307–31.

Kember, D. 1995. *Open learning courses for adults: A model of student progress*. Englewood Cliffs, NJ: Education Technology.

1999. Integrating part-time study with family, work and social obligations. *Studies in Higher Education*, 24(1), 109–24.

Kessler, C. and Idar, I. 1979. Acquisition of English by a Vietnamese mother and child. *Working Papers on Bilingualism*, 18, 65–80.

Kinginger, C. and Pavlenko A. 2002. Autobiographies of language learners: A course at the Summer Institute of Applied Linguistics. July 15 to July 26. Penn State.

Kouritzin, S. 2000a. A mother's tongue. *TESOL Quarterly* 34(2), 311–24.

2000b. Bringing life to research: Life history research and ESL. *TESL Canada Journal*, 17(2), 1–35.

2000c. Immigration mothers redefine access to ESL classes: Contradiction and ambivalence. *Journal of Multilingual and Multicultural Development*, 21(1), 14–19.

Lam, A. 2002. Language policy and learning experience in China: Six case histories. *Hong Kong Journal of Applied Linguistics*, 7(2), 57–72.

Lam, W. S. E. 2000. L2 literacy and the design of the self: A case study of a teenager writing on the Internet. *TESOL Quarterly*, 34(3), 457–82.

Lantolf, J. P. 1996. Second language acquisition theory-building: 'Letting all the flowers bloom!'. *Language Learning*, 46(4), 713–49.

Lantolf, J. P. and Pavlenko, A. 2001. (S)econd (L)anguage (A)ctivity theory: Understanding second language learners as people. In M. Breen (ed.), *Learner contributions to language learning: New directions in research* (pp. 141–58). London: Pearson Education.

Larsen-Freeman, D. 1983. Second language acquisition: Getting the whole picture. In K. M. Bailey, M. H. Long and S. Peck (eds.), *Second language acquisition studies* (pp. 3–22). Rowley, MA: Newbury House.

2001. Individual cognitive/affective learner contributions and differential success in second language acquisition. In M. P. Breen (ed.), *Learner contributions to language learning: New directions in research* (pp. 12–24). London: Longman.

Lave, J. and Wenger, E. 1991. *Situated learning: Legitimate peripheral participation.* Cambridge: Cambridge University Press.

Lazaraton, A. 2000. Current trends in research methodology and statistics in applied linguistics. *TESOL Quarterly*, 34(1), 175–81.

Leung, C-Y. 2002. Extensive reading and language learning: A diary study of a beginning learner of Japanese. *Reading in a Foreign Language*, 14(1), 66–81.

Lieblich, A., Tuval-Mashiach, R. and Zilber, T. 1998. *Narrative research: Reading, analysis and interpretation.* Thousand Oaks, CA: Sage.

Lightbown, P. and Spada, N. 1993. *How languages are learned.* Oxford: Oxford University Press.

Lim, H-Y. 2002. The interaction of motivation, perception and environment: One EFL learner's experience. *Hong Kong Journal of Applied Linguistics*, 7(2), 91–106.

Lin, A., Wang, W., Akamatsu, N. and Riazi, A. M. 2002. Appropriating English, expanding identities, and re-visioning the field: From TESOL to Teaching English for Glocalized Communication (TEGCOM). *Journal of Language, Identity and Education*, 1(4), 295–316.

Locke, E. A. and Latham, G. P. 1990. *A theory of goal setting and task performance.* Englewood Cliffs, NJ: Prentice Hall.

Long, M. H. 1990. The least a second language acquisition theory needs to explain. *TESOL Quarterly*, 24(4), 649–66.

1997. Construct validity in SLA research: A response to Firth and Wagner. *Modern Language Journal*, 81(3), 318–23.

Lvovich, N. 1997. *The multilingual self: An enquiry into language learning.* Mahwah, NJ: Lawrence Erlbaum.

Lyle, J. and Ogawa, D. M. 1990. Kokusai Kouryuu Kikin Terebi Nihongo Kouza 'Let's Learn Japanese' Hawai ni okeru shichousha no ankeeto chousa ('Let's Learn Japanese' – The questionnaire survey to the audience in Hawaii). *Nihongo Kyouiku Tsuushin*, 2, 22–3.

Marinova-Todd, S. H., Marshall, D. B. and Snow, C. E. 2000. Three misconceptions about age and L2 learning. *TESOL Quarterly*, 34(1), 9–43.

2001. Missing the point: A response to Hyltenstam and Abrahamsson. *TESOL Quarterly,* 35(1), 171–6.

McKay, S. and Wong, S-L. 1996. Multiple discourses, multiple identities: Investment and agency in second-language learning among Chinese adolescent immigrant students. *Harvard Educational Review*, 66(3), 577–608.

Miles, M. B. and Huberman, A. M. 1984. *Qualitative data analysis: A sourcebook of new methods.* London: Sage.

1994. *Qualitative data analysis: An expanded sourcebook.* 2nd edition. London: Sage.

## References

Morrow, N. 1997. Language and identity: Women's autobiographies of the American immigrant experience. *Language and Communication*, 17(3), 177–85.

Murphey, T. 1993. Why don't teachers learn what learners learn? Taking the guesswork out with Action Logging. *English Teaching Forum*. Washington DC USIS. January 1993, 6–10.

 (ed.) 1997. *Language learning histories*. Nagoya: South Mountain Press.

 (ed.) 1998a. *Language learning histories I*. Nagoya: South Mountain Press. Second printing of 1997 edition above, slightly edited.

 (ed.) 1998b. *Language learning histories II*. Nagoya: South Mountain Press.

 1998c. Friends and classroom identity formation. *IATEFL Issues*, 145, 15–16.

 1998d. Motivating with near peer role models. In *On JALT97: Trends and transitions* (pp. 201–5). Tokyo: JALT.

 1998e. *Language hungry!* Tokyo: Macmillan Language House.

 1999. Publishing students' language learning histories: For them, their peers, and their teachers. *Between the Keys*. Newsletter of the JALT Materials Writers SIG JALT, 7(2), 8–11, 14.

 2003. *Near peer role modeling*. NFLRC Video #14. Honolulu: University of Hawaii Second Language Teaching and Curriculum Center, presentation recorded 29 August 2002. http://nflrc.hawaii.edu/publication_home.cfm

Murphey, T. and Arao, H. 2001. Changing reported beliefs through near peer role modeling. *TESL-EJ*, 53, 1–15.

Murphey, T. and Murakami, H. 2001. Identifying and 'identifying with' effective beliefs and behaviors. *NLP World*, 8(3), 41–56.

Murphey, T. and Woo, L. 1998. Using student feedback for emerging lesson plans. *English Teachers Association of Switzerland Newsletter*, 15(2), 22–9.

Murray, D. E. 1996. The tapestry of diversity in our classrooms. In K. M. Bailey and D. Nunan (eds.), *Voices from the language classroom* (pp. 434–48). Cambridge: Cambridge University Press.

Naiman, N., Fröhlich, M., Stern, H. H. and Todesco, A. 1978. *The good language learner*. Research in Education Series No. 7. Ontario Institute for Studies in Education.

Newcombe, L. P. 2002. 'A tough hill to climb alone': Welsh learners speak. *Hong Kong Journal of Applied Linguistics*, 7(2), 39–56.

NHK 2002. *NHK Tekisuto Gaido* Guide to NHK textbooks. Tokyo: NHK.

Norton, B. 2000. *Identity and language learning: Gender, ethnicity and educational change*. London: Longman.

 2001. Non-participation, imagined communities and the language classroom. In Breen, M. (ed.), *Learner contributions to language learning: New directions in research* (pp. 159–71). London: Pearson Education.

Norton, B. and Toohey, K. 2001. Changing perspectives on good language learners. *TESOL Quarterly*, 35(2), 307–22.

Nunan, D. 1992. *Research methods in language learning*. Cambridge: Cambridge University Press.

Ogulnick, K. 1998. *Onna rashiku (Like a woman): The diary of a language learner in Japan*. Albany, NY: State University of New York Press.

(ed.) 2000. *Language crossings: Negotiating the self in a multicultural world.* New York: Teachers College Press.

Ohkushi, Y. 1991. Kouza bangumi wa dono you ni riyou sareteiru ka sono 2. – riyou no jittai (How are educational broadcasts used 2?: The actual conditions observed in the survey of use of educational broadcasts). NHK monthly report on broadcast research, December, 48–57.

Ohkushi, Y. and Hara, Y. 1991. Kouza bangumi wa dono you ni riyou sareteiru ka sono 1. – riyou no joukyou (How are educational broadcasts used 1?: An overview of the survey of use of educational broadcasts). NHK monthly report on broadcast research, October, 38–47.

Oxford, R. L. 1990. *Language learning strategies: What every teacher should know.* Rowley, MA: Newbury House.

1996. When emotion meets metacognition in language learning histories. *International Journal of Educational Research*, 23(7), 581–94.

Oxford, R. L. and Green, J. 1996. Language learning histories: Learners and teachers helping each other understand learning styles and strategies. *TESOL Journal*, 5(1), 20–3.

Oxford, R. L., Lavine, R. Z., Felkins, G., Hollaway, M. E. and Saleh, A. 1996. Telling their stories: Language students use diaries and recollections. In R. L. Oxford (ed.), *Language learning strategies around the world: Cross-cultural perspectives* (pp. 19–34). Honolulu: University of Hawaii.

Oxford, R. L. and Shearin, J. 1994. Language learning motivation: Expanding the theoretical framework. *Modern Language Journal*, 78, 12–28.

Pavlenko, A. 1998. Second language learning by adults: Testimonies of bilingual writers. *Issues in Applied Linguistics*, 9(1), 3–19.

2001a. 'How am I to become a woman in an American vein?': Transformations of gender performance in second language learning. In A. Pavlenko, A. Blackledge, I. Piller and M. Teutsch-Dwyer (eds.), *Multilingualism, second language learning, and gender* (pp. 133–73). Berlin: Mouton de Gruyter.

2001b. 'In the world of the tradition, I was unimagined': Negotiation of identities in cross-cultural autobiographies. *International Journal of Bilingualism*, 53, 317–44.

2001c. Language learning memoirs as a gendered genre. *Applied Linguistics*, 22(2), 213–40.

2002. Narrative study: Whose story is it, anyway? *TESOL Quarterly*, 36, 213–18.

Pavlenko, A. and Lantolf, J. P. 2000. Second language learning as participation and the (re)construction of selves. In J. P. Lantolf (ed.), *Sociocultural theory and second language learning* (pp. 155–78). Oxford: Oxford University Press.

Pavlenko, A. and Norton, B. forthcoming. Imagined communities, identity, and English language teaching. In J. Cummins and C. Davison (eds.), *Kluwer handbook of English language teaching*. Kluwer Academic.

Pennington, M. 1998. The teachability of phonology in adulthood: A re-examination. *International Review of Applied Linguistics*, 36(4), 323–42.

# References

Pennycook, A. 1990. Toward a critical applied linguistics for the 1990s. *Issues in Applied Linguistics*, 1, 8–28.

Polanyi, L. 1995. Language learning and living abroad: Stories from the field. In B. F. Freed (ed.), *Second language acquisition in a study abroad context* (pp. 271–91). Amsterdam: John Benjamins.

Polkinghorne, D. E. 1988. *Narrative knowing and the human sciences*. Albany, NY: State University of New York Press.

Rampton, B. 1991. Second language learners in a stratified multilingual setting. *Applied Linguistics*, 12(3), 229–48.

  1997. Second language research in late modernity: A response to Firth and Wagner. *Modern Language Journal*, 81(3), 329–33.

Riessman, C. K. 1993. *Narrative analysis*. Newbury Park, CA: Sage.

Rivers, W. M. 1964. *The psychologist and the language teacher*. Chicago: University of Chicago Press.

  1979. Learning a sixth language: An adult learner's daily diary. *Canadian Modern Language Review*, 36(1), 67–82.

Roberts, B. 2002. *Biographical research*. Buckingham, UK: Open University Press.

Rogoff, B., Paradise, R., Mejia Arauz, R., Correa-Chavez, M. and Angelillo, C. 2003. Firsthand learning through intent participation. *Annual Review of Psychology*, 54, 175–203.

Rubin, J. 1975. What the 'good language learner' can teach us. *TESOL Quarterly*, 9, 41–51.

Rustin, M. 2000. Reflections on the biographical turn in social science. In P. Chamberlayne, J. Bornat and T. Wengraf (eds.), *The turn to biographical methods in social science: Comparative issues and examples* (pp. 33–52). London: Routledge.

Rybak, S. 1980. *Learning languages from the BBC: Research into courses for adults*. London: BBC Education.

  1983. Foreign languages by radio and television: The development of a support strategy for adult home-learners. PhD thesis, Brighton Polytechnic.

Sakui, K. 2002. Swiss cheese syndrome: Knowing myself as a learner and teacher. *Hong Kong Journal of Applied Linguistics*, 7(2), 136–51.

Sataporn, S. 2000. Learners' behaviours and their personal culture of learning English in a self-instructional English programme at an open university in Thailand. PhD thesis, University of Leeds.

Sawyer, R. K. 2002. Emergence in psychology: Lessons from the history of non-reductionist science. *Human Development*, 45, 2–28.

Schmidt, R. 1983. Interaction, acculturation and the acquisition of communicative competence: A case study of an adult. In N. Wolfson and E. Judd (eds.), *Sociolinguistics and language acquisition* (pp. 137–74). Rowley, MA: Newbury House.

Schmidt, R. and Frota, S. 1986. Developing basic conversational ability in a second language: A case study of an adult learner of Portuguese. In R. Day (ed.), *Talking to learn* (pp. 237–326). Rowley, MA: Newbury House.

Schumann, F. M. 1980. Diary of a language learner: A further analysis. In R.

Scarcella and S. Krashen (eds.), *Research in second language acquisition: Selected papers of the Los Angeles Second Language Research Forum* (pp. 51–7). Rowley MA: Newbury House.

Schumann, F. M. and Schumann, J. H. 1977. Diary of a language learner: An introspective study of second language learning. In H. D. Brown, C. A. Yorio and R. Crymes (eds.), *On TESOL '77 teaching and learning English as a second language: Trends in research and practice* (pp. 241–9). Washington, DC: TESOL.

Schumann, J. H. 1978a. Second language acquisition: The pidginization hypothesis. In E. M. Hatch (ed.), *Second language acquisition: A book of readings* (pp. 256–71). Rowley, MA: Newbury House.

1978b. The acculturation model for second-language acquisition. In R. Gingras (ed.), *Second language acquisition and foreign language teaching* (pp. 27–50). Arlington, VA: Center for Applied Linguistics.

1997. *The neurobiology of affect in language learning*. Oxford: Blackwell.

Schunk, D. H. 1990. Goal setting and self-efficacy during self-regulated learning. *Educational Psychologist*, 25, 71–86.

Schunk, D. H. and Zimmerman, B. 1997. Developing self-efficacious readers and writers: The role of social and self-regulatory processes. In J. Guthrie and A. Wigfield (eds.), *Reading engagement: Motivating readers through integrated instruction* (pp. 34–50). Newark, Delaware: Reading Association.

Scovel, T. 2001. *Learning new languages: A guide to second language acquisition*. Boston, MA: Heinle and Heinle.

Shapira, R. G. 1978. The non-learning of English: A case study of an adult. In E. M. Hatch (ed.), *Second language acquisition: A book of readings* (pp. 246–55). Rowley, MA: Newbury House.

Shen, F. 1989. The classroom and the wider culture: Identity as a key to learning English composition. *College Composition and Communication*, 40, 459–66.

Sherer, K. R. 2000. Emotions as episodes of subsystem synchronization driven by nonlinear appraisal processes. In M. D. Lewis and I. Granic (eds.), *Emotion, development, and self-organization: Dynamic systems approaches to emotional development* (pp. 70–99). Cambridge: Cambridge University Press.

Siegel, J. 2003. Social context. In C. J. Doughty and M. H. Long (eds.), *The handbook of second language acquisition* (pp. 178–223). Oxford: Blackwell.

Singleton, D. 1989. *Language acquisition: The age factor*. Clevedon: Multilingual Matters.

Singleton, D. M. and Lengyel, Z. (eds.) 1995. *The age factor in second language acquisition*. Clevedon: Multilingual Matters.

Skehan, P. 1989. *Individual differences in second-language learning*. London: Edward Arnold.

1991. Individual differences in second-language learning. *Studies in Second Language Acquisition*, 13, 275–98.

Skier, E. and Vye, S. 2003. One reality of autonomous language learning in

Japan: Time, shame, and maturity. In A. Barfield and M. Nix (eds.), *Autonomy you ask!* (pp. 27–40). Tokyo: The Learner Development SIG of JALT.

Slimani, A. 1989. The role of topicalisation in classroom language learning. *System*, 17(2), 223–34.

1992. Evaluation of classroom interaction. In C. Alderson and A. Beretta (eds.), *Evaluating second language education* (pp. 197–221). Cambridge: Cambridge University Press.

Smith, J. and Spurling, A. 2001. *Understanding motivation for lifelong learning.* Sandford: Southgate Publishers.

*SPAN 111 Introduction to the Spanish language. Course outline.* 1999. Wellington: Victoria University of Wellington.

Spolsky, B. 2000. Language motivation revisited. *Applied Linguistics*, 21(2), 157–69.

Stenhouse, L. 1983. The process of standards in illuminative research. In Bartelett, L. S. Kemmis and G. Gillard (eds.), *Perspectives on case study: The quasi-historical approach.* Geelong Victoria: Deakin University Press.

Sternberg, R. J. 1985. *Beyond IQ: A triarchic theory of human intelligence.* New York: Cambridge University Press.

1988. *The triarchic mind: A new theory of human intelligence.* New York: Viking Press.

Stevick, E. 1989. *Success with foreign languages: Seven who achieved it and what worked for them.* New York: Prentice Hall.

Stipek, D. J. 1996. Motivation and instruction. In D. C. Berliner and R. C. Calfee (eds.), *Handbook of educational psychology* (pp. 85–113). New York: Macmillan.

Swain, M. and Miccoli, L. S. 1994. Learning in a content-based, collaboratively-structured course: The experience of an adult ESL learner. *TESL Canada Journal*, 12(1), 15–28.

Sweet, H. 1899. *The practical study of languages: A guide for teachers and learners.* Oxford: Oxford University Press.

Sweet, R. 1986. Student dropout in distance education: An application of Tinto's model. *Distance Education*, 12, 201–13.

Tarone, E. 1997. Analyzing IL in natural settings: A sociolinguistic perspective on second-language acquisition. *Communication and Cognition*, 30(1–2), 137–49.

Teutsch-Dwyer, M. 2001. (Re)constructing masculinity in a new linguistic reality. In A. Pavlenko, A. Blackledge, I. Piller and M. Teutsch-Dwyer (eds.), *Multilingualism, second language learning, and gender* (pp. 175–98). Berlin: Mouton de Gruyter.

Thorpe, M. 1996. Evaluation and a culture of learning. In S. Brown and B. Smith (eds.), *Resource-based learning* (pp. 120–29). London: Kogan Page.

Toohey, K. 2000. *Learning English at school: Identity, social relations and classroom practice.* Clevedon: Multilingual Matters.

Tremblay, P. G. and Gardner, R. C. 1995. Expanding the motivation construct in language learning. *Modern Language Journal*, 79, 505–20.

Tse, L. 2000. Student perceptions of foreign language study: A qualitative analysis of foreign language autobiographies. *Modern Language Journal*, 84(1), 69–84.

Umino, T. 1999. The use of self-instructional broadcast materials for L2 learning: An investigation in the Japanese context. *System*, 27(3), 309–27.

2002. Foreign language learning with self-instructional television materials: An exploratory study. PhD dissertation, Institute of Education, University of London.

Ushioda, E. 1996. *Learner autonomy 5: The role of motivation*. Dublin: Authentik.

1998. Effective motivational thinking: A cognitive theoretical approach to the study of language learning motivation. In E. A. Soler and V. C. Espurz (eds.), *Current issues in English language methodology* (pp. 77–89). Castelló de la Plana, Spain: Universitat Jaume I.

2001. Language learning at university: Exploring the role of motivational thinking. In Z. Dörnyei and R. Schmidt (eds.), *Motivation and second language acquisition* (pp. 93–125). University of Hawaii: Second Language Teaching and Curriculum Center.

Vann, R. J. and Abraham, R. G. 1990. Strategies of successful learners. *TESOL Quarterly*, 24(2), 177–98.

Wajnryb, R. 1988. V is for vulnerability. *Prospect*, 3(3), 339–51.

Walker, E. 2004. Power shifts in a language learning career. *Hong Kong Journal of Applied Linguistics*, 9(2).

Wenden, A. L. 1986a. Helping language learners think about learning. *ELT Journal*, 40(1), 3–12.

1986b. What do second language learners know about their second language learning? A second look at retrospective learner accounts. *Applied Linguistics* 7(2), 186–201.

1987. How to be a successful language learner: Insights and prescriptions from L2 learners. In A. Wenden and J. Rubin (eds.), *Learner strategies in language learning* (pp. 103–14). London: Prentice Hall.

2002. Learner development in language learning. *Applied Linguistics*, 23(1), 32–55.

Wenger, E. 1998. *Communities of practice: Learning, meaning, and identity*. Cambridge, MA: Cambridge University Press.

Wentzel, K. R. 1999. Socio-motivational processes and interpersonal relationships: Implications for understanding motivation at school. *Journal of Educational Psychology*, 91, 76–97.

Wertsch, J. V. 1991. *Voices of the mind: A sociocultural approach to mediated action*. Cambridge, MA: Harvard University Press.

1998. *Mind as action*. New York/Oxford: Oxford University Press.

Wertsch, J. V., Tulviste, P. and Hagstrom F. 1993. A sociocultural approach to agency. In E. A. Forman, N. Minick and C. A. Stone (eds.), *Contexts for learning: Sociocultural dynamics in children's development* (pp. 336–56). Oxford: Oxford University Press.

White, C. 1999. Expectations and emergent beliefs of self-instructed language learners. *System*, 27(4), 443–57.

Wierzbicka, A. 1985. The double life of a bilingual. In R. Sussex and J.

Zubrzycki (eds.), *Polish people and culture in Australia* (pp. 187–223). Canberra: Australian National University.

Williams, M. and Burden, R. 1997. *Psychology for language teachers*. Cambridge: Cambridge University Press.

Woodley, A., de Lange, P. and Tanewski, G. 2001. Student progress in distance education: Kember's model re-visited. *Open Learning*, 16(2), 113–31.

Yamashita, Y. 1998. Near peer role modeling in language learning histories. Unpublished senior thesis in communication psychology at Nanzan University, Department of American and British Studies.

Yin, R. K. 1994. *Case study research: Design and methods*. Thousand Oaks, CA: Sage.

# Index

# Index